WHEN GOD HAPPENS

WHEN GOD HAPPENS

Angels, Miracles, and Heavenly Encounters

COLLECTED AND EDITED BY

ANGELA HUNT AND **BILL MYERS**

SALEM BOOKS
an imprint of Regnery Publishing

Regnery® is a registered trademark of Salem Communications Holding Corporation

Salem Books™ is a trademark of Salem Communications Holding Corporation

(NLT) Holy Bible, New Living Translation, copyright (C) 1996, 2004, 2015 by
     Tyndale House Foundation. Used by permission of Tyndale House Publishers,
     Inc., Carol Stream, Illinois 60188. All rights reserved.
Tree of Life (TLV) Translation of the Bible. Copyright (C) 2015
     by The Messianic Jewish Family Bible Society.
King James Version (KJV) Public Domain
(NCV) The Holy Bible, New Century Version (R). Copyright (C) 2005
     by Thomas Nelson, Inc.
(JNT) David H. Stern, editor, Lederer Messianic Publications; 1st edition
     (September 1, 1989)

Cataloging-in-Publication data on file with the Library of Congress

ISBN: 978-1-62157-890-1
Ebook ISBN: 978-1-62157-891-8

Library of Congress Cataloging-in-Publication Data

Published in the United States by
Salem Books, an imprint of
Regnery Publishing
A Division of Salem Media Group
300 New Jersey Ave NW
Washington, DC 20001
www.Regnery.com

Manufactured in the United States of America

2019 Printing

Books are available in quantity for promotional or premium use. For information on discounts and terms, please visit our website: www.Regnery.com

Sandra Byrd, Melody Carlson, April Chapman, Judy Combs, Brett Dewey, Beverly Fish, Shirlanne Gay-Alexander, Amber Horsman, Tracy McGarvey, Peggy Patrick Medberry, Christopher Moya, Bill Myers, Jennifer L. Porter, Marlene Rice, Tim Riter, Martha Rogers, Yvonne Vollertt-Noblitt/Caylen D. Smith, Bruce Van Natta, and Sarena Wellman

CONTENTS

"On many occasions, God has become especially real, and has sent His unseen angelic visitors to touch my body to let me be His messenger for heaven, speaking as a dying man to dying men."[1]

—Billy Graham

INTRODUCTION

I've always had a special interest in angels—after all, my first name comes from the same Greek word meaning *messenger.* I'd like to think my name is apt because I'm a writer who is constantly relaying messages through books, articles, and honey-do lists.

When I was growing up, I wanted to think I had a wee bit in common with the angels because I tried hard to be a good girl. Angels are good, aren't they? And aren't they beautiful? Who wouldn't want to be angelic?

But as I grew older, I learned what society believes about angels and what the Bible says about angels are vastly different. So, before you read through this collection of stories about modern people who've had angel encounters, you might find it helpful to review a biblical *who, what, when, where, how,* and *why* about angelic beings.

Who are angels? They are individual beings, with names, jobs, and designated classifications. Only two angels are named in the sixty-six books of the Bible: Gabriel and Michael. Others are known by their workplace location—"the angel of the abyss" (Rev. 9:11), for instance, and "the angel of the waters" (Rev. 16:5).

Angels have specific jobs, or duties. Their chief duty is to worship and serve God. Some are warriors who fight in God's army and defend God's people. Others are guardians of children. Others are messengers. Others are escorts who transport human souls from mortal life into eternity.

Angels also are also classified. *Cherubim* (plural of *cherub*) are not cute, winged babies with bows and arrows. They are special angels charged with guarding. Two cherubim were placed at the Garden of Eden to guard the tree of life after Adam and Eve were expelled from the garden. Two cherubim were depicted on top of the Ark of the Covenant as if to guard the holy place.

Seraphim, who were seen by Isaiah in a vision, hover above the throne of God and remind the onlooker that God is holy. The word *seraph*, the singular form, means *burning* and reminds us to have a burning devotion to God.

Archangels are probably "chief angels," high in rank and power. The only archangel named in the Bible is Michael. I'm sure there are other types of angels, and when we are in heaven we will doubtless learn all about them.

I've seen dozens of paintings and statues of angels with feminine faces and wearing gorgeous gowns, but of all the angels mentioned in the Bible, none is described as a woman or given a woman's name. All are described as mature men, and if they are named, they are given male names.

The Bible frequently mentions a unique angel known as the **angel of the LORD**. He is unique because men who meet him usually fall to the ground to worship and call him *Lord*. Who is this angel?

We first meet Him in Genesis 16, when Sarah treats Hagar so badly the slave runs away.

> The angel of the Lord found Hagar beside a spring of water in the wilderness, along the road to Shur. The angel said to her, "Hagar, Sarai's servant, where have you come from, and where are you going?" (Gen. 16:7–8, NLT)
>
> The angel of the Lord said to her, "Return to your mistress, and submit to her authority." Then he added, "I will give you more descendants than you can count."
>
> And the angel also said, "You are now pregnant and will give birth to a son. You are to name him Ishmael (which means 'God hears'), for the Lord has heard your cry of distress. This son of yours will be a wild man, as untamed as a wild donkey! He will raise his fist against everyone, and everyone will be against him. Yes, he will live in open hostility against all his relatives."
>
> Thereafter, Hagar used another name to refer to the Lord, who had spoken to her. She said, "You are the God who sees me." She also said, "Have I truly seen the One who sees me?" (Gen. 16:9–13, NLT).

Hagar meets an angel, but this angel is unlike any other. He sees the future, He is holy. In short, He is God-in-flesh. He is Christ before Bethlehem. In theological terms, these Old Testament appearances of God-in-flesh are known as *theophanies*, and the Scriptures are filled with them.

We see Him again in Genesis 22:11–12 when Abraham picks up a knife and is about to slay Isaac as a sacrifice:

> At that moment the angel of the Lord called to him from heaven, "Abraham! Abraham!"

"Yes," Abraham replied. "Here I am!"

"Don't lay a hand on the boy!" the angel said. "Do not hurt him in any way, for now I know that you truly fear God. You have not withheld *from me* even your son, your only son" (NLT, italics added).

Do you see? Abraham was sacrificing his son to God, and the Angel of the Lord said, "You have not withheld your only son from me"—speaking for God.

In Exodus 3, Moses met the angel of the LORD:

There the angel of the LORD appeared to him in a blazing fire from the middle of a bush. Moses stared in amazement. Although the bush was engulfed in flames, it didn't burn up. "This is amazing," Moses said to himself. "Why isn't that bush burning up? I must go see it."

When the Lord saw Moses coming to take a closer look, God called to him from the middle of the bush, "Moses! Moses!"

"Here I am!" Moses replied.

"Do not come any closer," the LORD warned. "Take off your sandals, for you are standing on holy ground. I am the God of your father—the God of Abraham, the God of Isaac, and the God of Jacob." When Moses heard this, he covered his face because he was afraid to look at God (Exod. 3:2–5, NLT).

In this passage, the Angel of the Lord expressly declares He is the God of Abraham, Isaac, and Jacob. And Moses is afraid to look at God.

So, when you read about "the angel of the LORD," you are reading about an Old Testament appearance of the Son of God, the second member of the triune Godhead. Notice, "*an* angel of the Lord" could be speaking about any holy angel, but "*the* angel of the Lord" refers to Christ.

The third member of the Godhead, the Holy Spirit, is also mentioned many times in the Old Testament, as early as Genesis 1:2: " . . . and the *Ruach Elohim* [Holy Spirit] was hovering upon the surface of the water" (TLV).

The Bible records several conversations between "the angel of the Lord" and the Lord God—they are two separate persons. Look at Zechariah 1:8–17:

> In a vision during the night, I saw a man sitting on a red horse that was standing among some myrtle trees in a small valley. Behind him were riders on red, brown, and white horses. I asked the angel who was talking with me, "My lord, what do these horses mean?"
>
> "I will show you," the angel replied.
>
> The rider standing among the myrtle trees then explained, "They are the ones the Lord has sent out to patrol the earth."
>
> Then the other riders reported to *the angel of the* LORD, who was standing among the myrtle trees, "We have been patrolling the earth, and the whole earth is at peace."
>
> Upon hearing this, *the angel of the* LORD prayed this prayer: "O Lord of Heaven's Armies, for seventy years now you have been angry with Jerusalem and the towns of Judah. How long until you again show mercy to them?" And *the* LORD spoke kind and comforting words to the angel who talked with me.
>
> Then the angel said to me, "Shout this message for all to hear: 'This is what the Lord of Heaven's Armies says: My love for Jerusalem and Mount Zion is passionate and strong . . .'" (NLT, emphasis added).

After the Son of God is born in Bethlehem, lives, dies, is resurrected, and returns to Heaven, He is no longer known as "the angel of the Lord," but as Jesus the Christ. So, references to "the angel of the Lord" are found only in the Old Testament.

What are angels? What are they like?

Angels are not the spirits of the people who were once human. Angels are unique beings who were created by God and his Son, and all the angels were created at one point in time. Through the inspiration of the Spirit, Paul wrote: "It is through his Son [Jesus] that we have redemption—that is, our sins have been forgiven. He is the visible image of the invisible God. He is supreme over all creation, because in connection with him were created all things—in heaven and on earth, visible and invisible, whether thrones, lordships, rulers or authorities—they have all been created through him and for him. He existed before all things, and he holds everything together" (Col. 1:14–17, JNT).

Jesus, the Son of God, is not and never has been an angel. He is the second person of the Trinity, and although he willingly placed himself "lower than the angels for a brief time," He is God.

> Hebrews spells out seven reasons why Christ is superior to angels. (1) He has a more excellent name than angels (1:4–5). He is the Son of God; angels are only God's servants, not His equals. (2) God's angels worship God's Son (1:6), and they are never to be worshiped. (3) God's angels are creatures created by God's Son who is the uncreated One (1:7). (4) The Father called God's Son "God," and even in His incarnate state, He had greater gifts than angels (1:8–9). (5) The angels are servants of God, but Christ is God's Son and the divine Servant of Yahweh (1:14). (6) The Word of God did not originate with angels. They were simply used of God

to give His message to man, whereas the word was spoken by "the Lord" (2:2–3). (7) In the future millennium, Christ, not angels, will rule (2:5–7).[2]

What are angels like? They are like humans in that they have intellect, will, and emotion. Angels do not know everything, for they are not omniscient like God. But they undoubtedly have a greater intellect than humans because they know all about the heavenlies, they have had access to all knowledge since their creation, and the holy angels have not suffered the corrupting effect of sin.

They have emotion, for the Bible tells us the angels rejoice when a human repents of his sin and turns to God. Their love is completely centered on God, for they worship and serve Him without ceasing.

Angels have will because they were given the freedom to choose holiness or unholiness at some point after their creation. Once they chose, they have been "sealed" or confirmed, and they do not change their minds.

Angels are eternal. They did have a beginning, but they do not have an end. They do not grow old or deteriorate like moral beings and earthly things.

Angels have great power, stronger than any human alive or dead.

Psalm 103:20 speaks of angels as being *mighty in strength*. In Matthew 28:2, only one angel was needed to roll away the stone from the tomb of Yeshua [Jesus], though normally, several men would have been needed to move such a stone. One angel *opened the prison doors* in Acts 5:19. In Acts 12:7, an angel was able to snap Peter's chains off in prison. An angel was able to smite Agrippa with a disease that would take his life in Acts 12:23.

Angels are referred to by the term *powers* in Ephesians 1:21; 3:10, and Colossians 1:16. 2 Thessalonians 1:7 speaks of the angels of his power, and 2 Peter 2:11 refers to the power of angels.[3]

When were the angels created?

God created the angels before He created the earth, mankind, or the animals:

> "Where were you when I laid the foundations of the earth?
> Tell me, if you know so much.
> Who determined its dimensions
> and stretched out the surveying line?
> What supports its foundations,
> and who laid its cornerstone
> as the morning stars sang together
> and all the angels shouted for joy? (Job 38:4–7, NLT)

The angels were created holy—sinless—but they were given the ability to choose contrary to their nature. They could choose unholiness, and one-third of them did. After this choice, all the angels were confirmed in their choices, and they will remain in their state of holiness or unholiness for eternity. The unholy angels will be consigned to the Lake of Fire after the Last Judgment.

The angels who chose to disobey God are now known as unholy angels. Some people call them *demons* or *fallen angels.* Lucifer—the devil, or Satan—is a fallen angel. "Yes," he [Jesus] told them, "I saw Satan fall from heaven like lightning!" (Matt. 10:18, NLT).

The unholy angels are active today, working to frustrate the plans of God. They tempt Christians, deceive and blind unbelievers, and destroy human lives. They are active in the drug trade, in pornography, and in the wholesale destruction of innocence.

The majority of the angels *did* choose to obey God, and they are known as the holy angels. "For if someone is ashamed of me and of what I say in this adulterous and sinful generation, the Son of Man also will be ashamed of him when he comes in his Father's glory with the holy angels" (Mark 8:38, JNT).

The holy angels are engaged in an invisible struggle against the unholy angels. Christians can engage in spiritual warfare, too, through prayer, obeying God, and realizing the struggle exists.

How many angels did God create? A large, finite number, probably higher than we can count.

> "The Lord came from Mount Sinai
> and rose like the sun from Edom;
> he showed his greatness from Mount Paran.
> He came with thousands of angels
> from the southern mountains (Deut. 33:2, NCV).

The chariots of God are twenty thousand, even thousands of angels: the Lord is among them, *as in* Sinai, in the holy *place* (Ps. 68:17, KJV).

"No, you have come to Mount Zion, to the city of the living God, the heavenly Jerusalem, and to countless thousands of angels in a joyful gathering" (Heb. 12:22, NLT).

Where do angels live? The holy angels live in Heaven.

"See that you never despise one of these little ones, for I tell you that their angels in heaven are continually seeing the face of my Father in heaven" (Matt. 18:10, JNT).

Angels live in Heaven, but they operate on earth and in "the heavenlies"—which may be another dimension. They often have special missions to accomplish in our world, and they battle ungodly spiritual entities on earth, in the heavenly places, and in other dimensions.

How do angels appear? Angels appear in three ways: First, they appear in dreams while people sleep. While Jacob slept, he saw angels going up and down a ladder that stretched to Heaven (Genesis 28:12).

Second, sometimes angels appear in visions when people are awake. Daniel, Zechariah, and John the Revelator saw angels in visions and received messages from them.

Third, sometimes angels manifest "out of thin air." Angels can assume human form, and they often do. They can disappear as quickly and unexpectedly as they appear.

Why did God create angels? If there are so many of them, why do we so rarely see them?

God created the angels because their creation was part of His holy will. He did not need them, He does not require them to survive or to do His work, but He chose to create them even knowing that some of them would exercise their freedom to choose unholiness.

Why do people sometimes see them? Although we cannot know every thought in the mind of God, through reading the biblical accounts, we can see God often sends an angel because an angel would elicit the best response from the human on the receiving end. The first reaction most folks have to seeing an angel—unless it's an angel who appears as a completely ordinary man—is complete and utter fear:

> David was terrified by the sword of the angel of the Lord (1 Chr. 21:30); Zechariah was afraid when he saw the angel (Luke 1:12); I was frightened and fell on my face (Dan. 8:17); a great trembling fell on them and they fled to hide themselves (Dan. 10:7); the guards were

afraid of the angel of the Lord (Matt. 28:4); they went from the tomb in fear and great joy (Matt. 28:8); trembling and astonishment had gripped them (Mark 16:8); they said nothing to anyone because they were afraid (Mark 16:8); Cornelius looked at the angel in terror (Acts 10:4).[4]

In other accounts, people didn't realize they encountered an angel until later. Balaam didn't know an angel was blocking his donkey's way (Num. 22:27). Abraham and Lot entertained angels (and Abraham entertained the Lord) without knowing who they were at first. The author of Hebrews warns us, "Don't forget to show hospitality to strangers, for some who have done this have entertained angels without realizing it!" (13:2, NLT).

God sends angels to encourage the people of God who are going through trials. When Jacob, who parted badly from his brother Esau, approached his brother's home with great fear and trepidation, God sent an entire host of angels to meet and encourage him (Gen. 32:1–2). And when Paul was on a storm-tossed ship in danger of sinking, he told the terrified sailors: "For this very night, there stood next to me an angel of the God to whom I belong and whom I serve. He said, 'Don't be afraid, Sha'ul! you have to stand before the Emperor. Look! God has granted you all those who are sailing with you.' So, men, take heart! For I trust God and believe that what I have been told will come true (Acts 27:23–25, JNT).

God sent an angel to a worried woman with a sprained ankle, assuring her she would be healed and ready to visit the Holy Land in ten days. In the same way, God sent an angel to comfort a frightened young missionary alone and friendless in a foreign airport.

God sends angels to deliver messages, just as he sent Gabriel to the Virgin Mary to tell her she would bear a child, the Son of

God. He sent an angel to Daniel to outline God's prophetic plan for creation, and He sent an angel to the apostle John to reveal even more information at the end of times, which John wrote down and we know as the book of Revelation.

God also used an angel to deliver a message to a discouraged Christian filmmaker who was about to walk away from his God-given calling.

God sends angels to deliver and save His people, just as he sent an angel to shut the mouths of the lions in a cave with Daniel—and a woman who was about to drown in a California riptide.

God sends angels to remind us the spiritual world is real. When the king of Aram came against the prophet Elisha, Elisha's servant saw the enemy army and their many chariots lined up outside the prophet's house.

> When the servant of the man of God got up early the next morning and went outside, there were troops, horses, and chariots everywhere. "Oh, sir, what will we do now?" the young man cried to Elisha.
>
> "Don't be afraid!" Elisha told him. "For there are more on our side than on theirs!" Then Elisha prayed, "O Lord, open his eyes and let him see!" The Lord opened the young man's eyes, and when he looked up, he saw the hillside around Elisha was filled with horses and chariots of fire. (2 Kings 6:15–17, NLT)

In the same way, God showed a young man heading into the ministry that a troubling recurrent dream was real and part of spiritual warfare, but that sort of evil could be defeated in Jesus' name.

God sends angels to set an example for us. They obey joyfully and instantly and honor God in all they do. They model reverence and holiness and remind us to do the same—just as a young housewife was reminded to demonstrate kindness to an unexpected visitor who was less than lovely.

God sends angels to escort dying humans into eternity (Luke 16:22)—just like the angel who touched a broken music box to help a granddaughter know her beloved grandmother was on her way to Heaven.

God allows angels to learn from the church. We think of angels as powerful and intelligent, and they are. But angels long to learn from redeemed sinners because they have waited and watched as God's plan for the redemption of mankind has unfolded. They were present when God cast Adam and Eve out of the Garden of Eden, and they heard God promise the seed of the woman would crush the head of the serpent (Gen. 3:15). They heard the prophets speak of the Messiah Who would come to reign and to suffer, to be a king and a baby. They announced the news to the shepherds keeping their flocks in the fields outside Bethlehem, they ministered to Jesus after His temptation in the wilderness (Mark 1:13), and they rolled away the stone over his tomb to show the world He had risen! They spoke to the disciples and the women, then they ministered to the apostles when they were imprisoned and beaten and persecuted for Christ's sake.

And, Peter writes,

> This salvation was something even the prophets wanted to know more about when they prophesied about this gracious salvation prepared for you. They wondered what time or situation the Spirit of Christ within them was talking about when he told them in advance about Christ's suffering and his great glory afterward.
>
> They were told that their messages were not for themselves, but for you. And now this Good News has been announced to you by those who preached in the power of the Holy Spirit sent from heaven. It is all so

wonderful that even the angels are eagerly watching these things happen. (1 Pet. 1:10–12, NLT)

Yet, as wonderful as angels are, we must never forget that many of their vast number chose unholiness and disobedience over holiness and obedience. Satan was a powerful cherub, but so great was his pride in his beauty and power he was cast out of Heaven and took one-third of the angels with him.

We cannot be so enamored with the idea of angels we forget some have set themselves against God. How can we tell them apart when the Bible says even Satan "masquerades as an angel of light" (2 Cor. 11:14)?

The following three principles will guide you in any possible interaction with an angel.

First, **we are not to seek, worship, or pray to angels**. Why would you seek out an angel instead of seeking God? Angels are not God; they are his servants. They do not answer prayers. So, do not seek out an angel or allow a fallen angel to enter your life.

> We are to pray only to God, who alone is omnipotent and thus able to answer prayer and who alone is omniscient and therefore able to hear the prayers of all his people at once. By virtue of omnipotence and omniscience, God the Son and God the Holy Spirit are also worthy of being prayed to, but this is not true of any other being. Paul warns us against thinking any other "mediator" can come between us and God, "for there is one God, and there is *one mediator* between God and men, the man Christ Jesus" (1 Tim. 2:5). If we were to pray to angels, it would be implicitly attributing to them a status equal to God, which we must not do. There is no example in Scripture of anyone praying to any specific angel or asking angels for help.[5]

Second, we must beware of any angel who teaches false doctrine. Paul wrote, "Let God's curse fall on anyone, including us or even an angel from heaven, who preaches a different kind of Good News than the one we preached to you" (Gal. 1:8 NLT). False angels lie and deceive. False religions and cults have been based on teachings from false angels.

The angel who spoke to John and gave him the book of Revelation said this:

> The Spirit and the bride say, "Come." Let anyone who hears this say, "Come." Let anyone who is thirsty come. Let anyone who desires drink freely from the water of life. And I solemnly declare to everyone who hears the words of prophecy written in this book: If anyone adds anything to what is written here, God will add to that person the plagues described in this book. And if anyone removes any of the words from this book of prophecy, God will remove that person's share in the tree of life and in the holy city that are described in this book. (Rev. 22:17–19 NLT)

If at any time you have an encounter with a being whom you suspect of being an angel, carefully consider his purpose in coming to you. Does he glorify God? Does he honor Jesus? Does he say or do anything contrary to Scripture?

Holy angels are real, and God may send one to help you in a time of trouble. Live, therefore, in such a way that your activities, words, and actions will make His heart joyful and glorify our Father in Heaven. The angels—seen or unseen—will praise God, too!

—Angela Hunt, Th.D.

CHAPTER ONE

ANGEL ON MY DOORSTEP

MARTHA ROGERS

In the summer of 1960, my husband and I lived in a middle-class neighborhood of older homes and duplexes. Ours was a two-story duplex, and we lived on the bottom floor. The couple upstairs worked and were gone during the day, so I had the place all to myself.

I was a newlywed home economist for the electric utility company in Houston, Texas. Because my duties included conducting cooking schools and demonstrating food preparation, I often worked at home to create the recipes I would use in my classes and demonstrations.

At least once a week, I experimented with recipes I found in newspapers, magazines, and old cookbooks.

One morning, I was working at home alone, concocting foods for a two-hour cooking school the next day. I tested several main dishes, including meatloaf, spaghetti sauce, lasagna, and a chicken casserole. My menus also included vegetables, salads, breads, and desserts.

My casserole dishes, pans, serving dishes, platters, and cooling racks held more food than one can imagine for a single home kitchen. The place looked more like a restaurant. Food covered the counters and tables as well as space in the tiny breakfast alcove and dining room. I stashed the cold items—like a delicious congealed salad—in the refrigerator. I even whipped up two meat fillings to make sandwiches for my husband.

I tasted and sampled and decided which recipes I'd keep and which ones I'd toss. Exhausted, I finally took a break sometime after noon and ate a sandwich. I fixed a pitcher of tea for our dinner that night and poured a glass for my lunch.

Little did I know that within the hour, I would learn about deep-seated feelings I would have denied having. They came to the surface that day and taught me a lesson I will never forget.

Someone knocked on my door. I hesitated to answer it because I was alone. Then curiosity took over. After all, it could be the mailman or a deliveryman with a package, and I sure didn't want to miss that.

Most of the older houses in our neighborhood had screen doors back then, so I could open the front door and peek out through a locked screen door. When I did, an elderly black man in tattered overalls and a torn, dingy shirt stood on the other side. Worn-out shoes covered his sockless feet. His gray hair was matted, and he looked like he hadn't shaved in several days. The odor emanating from his body almost knocked me over, and I had to swallow hard to keep from gagging.

I peered at him through the screen door. "Can I help you?"

He bobbed his head and twisted an old hat in his hands. "Yes'm, could you spare an old man somethin' to eat? I shore is hungry. Anything at all would do."

Being alone, I was afraid to open the door to a stranger, especially one who smelled and looked as bad as he did. I really didn't want him on my porch.

"I'm sorry, but I have nothing to help you today. You'll have to try someone else."

His head bent forward and his shoulders sagged. He set his hat back on his head. "Thank you, ma'am." With that, he turned and shuffled off the porch.

I watched until he was down the steps and on the street because I wanted to be sure he was leaving.

When I went back to my kitchen, the sight of all those dishes was like a slap to my face. That room held enough food for a small army. Guilt poured over me like a wave—I gasped as if I were drowning. What was I *thinking*? I told that man an outright lie.

Words from Jesus' own lips filled my head. He talked about being fed when He was hungry and when His disciples asked when they did that, He told them, "Whatever you did for one of the least of these brothers, you did it for me."

Boy, was I convicted. I turned away a man in need when I had plenty to give away. Which left me with only one thing to do, share what I had.

I put together a lunch from the bounty on my table and counters. I made a sandwich from the fillings I prepared, wrapped two baked chicken breasts in foil, did the same for six chocolate-chip cookies, and filled a jar with milk. To the growing pile of food, I added a bag of chips from my pantry. I also added a plastic fork, spoon, and napkin.

After I found a shopping bag in the pantry, I filled it with the food. I still had a bit of room, so I added a few more cookies, another sandwich, a slice of pound cake, and a banana. I then went out to my car. I prayed the man was still somewhere in the neighborhood.

Only fifteen minutes had passed since he left my porch, so I figured he had to be close. After a few minutes, I spotted him and hurried to catch up with him. I stopped the car and rolled down my window. When I called out, he stopped and stared at me.

When I called to him the second time, he came over.

"I'm so sorry, but I do have plenty of food, and I brought this to share it with you." I gave him the bag.

The smile on his face at that moment was brighter than crown jewels glistening in sunlight. "Thank you, ma'am." He hefted the bag and smiled again. "Sure is heavy. Must be some good eatin' in here."

Those words held more sincere thanks than I'd ever heard. I looked into the face of someone who had pure gratefulness for something that had been easy for me to do.

He backed away and headed for the steps at the end of a sidewalk leading to a home. In our neighborhood, the yards were elevated, so three or four steps carried a pedestrian from the street sidewalk to the pathway leading to the home.

He sat on the top step and opened the bag. He spread the napkin on his lap, reached into the bag, and brought out a sandwich and the jar of milk. He set the milk beside him and unwrapped the sandwich.

As he began to eat, tears filled my eyes at the expression of joy on his face. Satisfied he would no longer be hungry—at least for a while—I pulled up into the next driveway to turn around and head home. I glanced over to him, and he waved at me. I waved back and completed my maneuver to turn around.

Back on the street, I looked up to wave goodbye, but he was nowhere to be seen. My mouth dropped open, and I blinked.

Nothing was on that top step. No man, no jar, no sack—nothing. He'd vanished into thin air. It couldn't have taken me more than a minute to turn around in that driveway, but my unexpected visitor was gone.

With my heart pounding and hands shaking, I drove all over the neighborhood. After fifteen minutes of cruising around the block and up another street, I finally gave up. I never saw the man again.

By this time, I was a nervous wreck. When I arrived home, I sat at my kitchen table and wept. All I could think about was how the man disappeared. Then I began to think about what feeding him did to my conscience and my heart. Was that old man a messenger from God?

What if I hadn't gone after him? What if I held onto my fear? I shuddered with the thought of failure. Then a voice seemed to speak to me, and I realized I *hadn't* failed. I *had* answered the call. A little late, perhaps, but I did answer.

What a blessing I would have missed and how disappointed God would have been had I stayed in my kitchen and put that old man's need out of my mind.

With renewed energy, I went about finishing my work.

That little encounter emphasized what I already knew but didn't practice. Helping others, no matter what, is helping Jesus do His work. I am not to judge anyone by their outward appearance, race, or background. I must be available and willing to help whenever God calls.

I firmly believe that man was an angel sent to help me learn a priceless lesson. God's plan worked because it changed this young newlywed's attitude. All these years later, I still remember the incident and thank the Lord for it. Not judging people has led me to some of the sweetest, kindest people I've ever known.

These days, I'm a writer, and when I was contracted to write a Christmas story, I thought of that day in my kitchen. I used an old man in tattered clothes and reeking with body odor to be the "angel" who saves the town of Stoney Creek after disaster strikes and gives it the best Christmas the residents have ever known. It all happens because the hero of the story sees something besides a tattered old man and takes him home, where his family accepts him without question and gives him food, clothing, and a place to live.

Maybe that's a lesson we all need to learn. Because sometimes, the stranger you serve was actually sent to serve *you*.

Martha Rogers is a novelist who lives in Houston with her husband Rex. Martha is a retired English teacher, and she and Rex spend their free time with church friends and visiting grandchildren and great-grandchildren. Martha is a graduate of Baylor University and a Bible study teacher, a health and nutrition instructor, and member of the choir at her church.

ANGEL GLIMPSES

My father, when he was a small boy, was climbing on an upper story of a house that was being built. He walked to the end of a board that was not nailed at the other end, and it slowly began to tip. He knew that he was doomed, but inexplicably the board began to tip the other way, as though a hand had pushed it down again. He always wondered if it was an angel's hand.[6]

—Elizabeth Elliott

CHAPTER TWO

SAVED BY ANGELS

BRUCE VAN NATTA

The events of November 16, 2006, changed my life forever; the experience will be with me as long as I live. Many of us can think of defining moments in our lives. Sometimes they are marked by tragedy, sometimes by triumph. Rarely are they marked by both. But this was one of those uncommon days.

I was a self-employed diesel mechanic who performed on-site repairs. On this particular day, I was at a customer's shop about forty-five minutes from my home. The vehicle I was working on was a Peterbilt logging truck. I worked nearly twelve hours that day to complete my portion of the engine, and I was just finishing. I worked with the driver of the truck, and after we put the engine back together, we began checking it over and testing the repairs. The rest of the truck was not yet completely reassembled because the driver planned on finishing the remaining work the next day.

I began to put my tools back into the toolboxes on my service truck as the semi engine ran up to operating temperature. The driver asked, because I was there, if I could also diagnose a non-related oil leak before I left. I was in a hurry to get home, but I thought the task would take only a few minutes. I rolled beneath the front of the truck feet-first on the creeper and started wiping the areas that appeared to be leaking. Then, without warning, the truck fell off the jack and crushed me against the concrete floor. The front axle fell across my midsection like a blunt guillotine, nearly cutting me in two. From my viewpoint, it looked and felt like I was cut in half.

In a moment of panic, I tried to bench press the 10,000-plus pounds mass off my chest. When reality set in, I realized the gravity of the situation and called out, "God, help me! God, help me!"

Through a haze of pain and bewilderment, I heard the truck driver call 911. When he got off the phone, I asked him to shut off the engine because the vibrations were transmitted through the axle and straight into my body. Small amounts of blood leaked from my mouth when I tried to talk. I watched the driver reposition the jack to raise the truck off my body. I was scared of the monster machine falling again, and I wanted to get away from that truck. The large chrome front bumper was just behind my head, and I reached both hands back and grabbed the bottom of it. It took all the strength I had to pull myself far enough that my head was out from under the truck. I stayed conscious long enough to see the first person who responded to the 911 call.

The next thing I remember, I was at least ten or fifteen feet above the scene, looking down at the whole situation. The strangest part of my out-of-body experience was feeling like I was only an observer to what was happening below me. It was as if I was watching a movie. I felt no emotion, only a sense of peace. I heard one man say there was no way I was going to live, and it didn't matter to me one way or another. From my viewpoint, I could tell my body was still mostly under the truck, but my head was sticking out past the front bumper. I could see my eyes were closed and my head was turned toward the driver's side of the truck. The man I was working with was on his knees behind me, crying and patting my head as he talked to me. I could hear and understand every word.

The most incredible thing wasn't that I was having this experience; it was what I saw next. On either side of my body were twin angels, also on their knees and facing the front of the truck. My vantage point was above and behind them. The driver of the truck was over six feet tall, yet the heads of these angels were at least a foot and a half higher than his head. Were they standing, I think they would've been close to eight feet tall. They had very broad shoulders and looked to be extremely muscular. They did not have wings. The angels had ringlets of long blonde hair that fell at least halfway down their backs. They were wearing white or ivory robes. It was hard to tell the exact color because of the yellowish light surrounding each angel. They seem to be glowing. I also noticed the robe fabric was unusual. It was a woven material, but the thread size was large, like miniature rope. It appeared to be very strong and durable. The Angels never moved; they were as steady as statues. I couldn't see their faces because my view came from behind them, but from what I could see, they were identical in appearance. Each angel kept his arms positioned under the truck, angled toward my body.

More people began to arrive at the scene of the accident, and I continued to watch from above. A red-haired emergency worker arrived, talked to someone, and walked up to the driver's side of the truck. She moved the truck driver out of the way and asked him my name. She held my head, patted my cheeks, and told me to open my eyes. She kept repeating herself in a loud voice, and the next thing I knew, I was no longer watching from above but was looking at her through my own eyes. She told me it was very important for me to keep my eyes open. I thought about what she was saying and realized I had been out of my body until she got me to open my eyes. This made me believe what she said was true and important; I was on the verge of death. Then I thought about the angels I saw. I looked at the spot where I saw them, but I could see nothing there with my human eyes.

As I lay on the floor, I heard a voice in my head telling me to shut my eyes and just give up. When I did shut my eyes, the incredible pain stopped, and I could feel my spirit drifting away from my body. But I also heard another voice, and this one was quieter, more like a whisper. It told me if I wanted to live, I would have to fight, and it would be a hard fight. It was almost as if the red-haired emergency worker could hear that voice, too, because she asked me what I had to fight for. All I could think of was my wife and four children.

These two voices, or conflicting thoughts, volleyed back and forth in my head. If you think of that old cartoon with the devil on one shoulder and an angel on the other, you can picture what was happening. The louder voice telling me to give up and die was not from God, but the whispering voice telling me to fight was. As always, the devil promotes death, and God promotes life. And God will always tell us the truth. He warned me it was going to be a hard fight, and it has been. Most often, I've found the right choice is not the easy one.

I was transported by ambulance to a local hospital and then flown to our state's largest trauma center. I stayed awake the whole time, fighting to hang on and refusing to close my eyes. When the emergency doctors started scanning my body, they were astounded. There were so many injuries they couldn't decide where to start or what to do. They gave me several units of blood, but it just kept leaking into my stomach cavity. As they were sliding me in for another CAT scan, everything started to go dim for me. Although I hadn't been able to talk for quite a while, the Lord gave me the strength to tell them I was going to die, and they had to do something right *now*. The doctors told me weeks later that as soon as I said that, my blood pressure dropped out of sight. They removed me from the machine and rushed me to the operating room.

The doctors operated only long enough to reattach the severed veins and arteries. The head trauma surgeon was called in from home. He told my family that in all his years as a trauma doctor, he never saw anybody so badly traumatized and still alive. He told my family he was going to cross his fingers and wait at least six hours to see if I was still alive before he would operate on me again. My wife told him he could cross his fingers, but that she and others were going to pray for my life. Their prayers were answered, and the doctors resumed operating on me the next morning. They had to remove most of my small intestine and perform various other repairs to combat several internal injuries. They decided not to do anything with the two spider-cracked vertebrae; they would try to let them heal on their own.

The next thing I remember was waking up a few weeks later. I had three operations during that time, and my wife never left my side. The night of my accident, she was at our children's school for parent-teacher conferences. When she got home and heard the news, she dropped to her knees and turned it all over to God, knowing He would give her the strength to get through whatever lay ahead. The only thing she took with her to the hospital that night was her Bible. To everyone's amazement, I went home from the hospital a little more than a month after the accident. But after a few days, I went back to the hospital with severe complications stemming from a damaged pancreas and spleen.

I spent a few more weeks in the hospital, but I got out long enough to spend the Christmas holidays at home. Then I returned to the hospital. This cycle repeated a few times, then the doctors decided they would have to perform another major operation. They had to remove another dead section of my small intestine that was almost completely closed off. We were told an adult needs a minimum of 100 centimeters of small intestine to be able to live by eating regular food. I was already down to this critical minimum length before my fourth operation, and then they removed more. Before the accident, I weighed more than 180 pounds; three months afterward, I was down to 126 pounds because of the inadequate amount of small intestine left in my body.

Nine months after the accident, I was at the hospital for some tests in preparation for my fifth operation. While performing the procedure, the radiologist and his supervisor found I had around 200 centimeters of small intestine. They couldn't imagine where the extra length came from.

When they looked at the doctors' notes from the previous operations, they found those doctors recorded a total length of 100 centimeters several times during the first three operations and removed more in my fourth procedure. They could not believe the head of the trauma department and other skilled doctors made multiple mistakes on my chart and in their calculations.

But I believe they didn't make mistakes, and here is why: what the radiologist didn't know was several people were praying for me, and a man named Bruce Carlson flew in from New York to pray over me after my fourth operation. This man has often displayed the gift of healing, and the Lord has used him to heal hundreds of people. The Bible tells us we Christians are to pray with the expectation of sick people being healed. Sometimes, God chooses not to heal someone in the method or timetable we want, but that is His decision, not ours. As believers, we are told to pray and leave the results up to God.

When Bruce Carlson prayed over me that day, he put one of his palms on my forehead. He asked the Lord to answer all the prayers people were praying for me, and when he said that, I felt something like electricity flow from his palm and into my body. He prayed for my small intestine to supernaturally grow in length in the name of Jesus, and as he did, I could feel something wiggle around inside my stomach. Of course, I didn't know for sure my intestine lengthened until the radiologist told me a few months later.

It has now been several years since my accident, and the doctors can't tell me exactly what all the long-term effects are going to be. I believe they will be minimal. There are still a few symptoms I deal with on a daily basis, but I keep getting better. My weight has also climbed back up to about 160 pounds, thanks to the added intestine.

Now that more time has passed, the doctors have also told me just what a miracle it is I am alive. They said because the artery and veins were completely severed, I should have bled to death internally in about eight to ten minutes. Rather, it was more than two and a half hours from the time I was injured until they started to operate on me. They also told me I am the only patient they have ever had at the hospital or anywhere else who has sustained these injuries and lived—all other patients have come in dead on arrival. I told my doctors I know why I'm still alive: I got to see the two angels that saved my life!

Adapted from *Saved by Angels* by Bruce Van Natta, published by Destiny Image Publishers, 2008. Used by permission.

Bruce Van Natta has been sent on a mission from Jesus to start fires in people's hearts for God. Since being crushed under a semi-truck and having an out-of-body experience where he witnessed angels the Lord sent, he has gone into full-time ministry. Through Sweet Bread Ministries, he shares his gripping testimony worldwide and loves to see people get saved, healed, set free, and delivered by the power and love of Jesus.

ANGEL GLIMPSES

Genesis 28:11–22 tells us the story of Jacob, who glimpsed a literal "stairway to heaven" when he was traveling to Haran.

> [11] At sundown he arrived at a good place to set up camp and stopped there for the night. Jacob found a stone to rest his head against and lay down to sleep. [12] As he slept, he dreamed of a stairway that reached from the earth up to heaven. And he saw the angels of God going up and down the stairway.
>
> [13] At the top of the stairway stood the Lord, and he said, "I am the Lord, the God of your grandfather Abraham, and the God of your father, Isaac. The ground you are lying on belongs to you. I am giving it to you and your descendants. [14] Your descendants will be as numerous as the dust of the earth! They will spread out in all directions—to the west and the east, to the north and the south. And all the families of the earth will be blessed through you and your descendants. [15] What's more, I am with you, and I will protect you wherever you go. One day I will bring you back to this land. I will not leave you until I have finished giving you everything I have promised you."
>
> [16] Then Jacob awoke from his sleep and said, "Surely the Lord is in this place, and I wasn't even aware of it!" [17] But he was also afraid and said, "What an awesome place this is! It is none other than the house of God, the very gateway to heaven!"
>
> [18] The next morning Jacob got up very early. He took the stone he had rested his head against, and he set it upright as a memorial pillar. Then he poured olive oil

over it. [19] He named that place Bethel (which means "house of God"), although it was previously called Luz.

[20] Then Jacob made this vow: "If God will indeed be with me and protect me on this journey, and if he will provide me with food and clothing, [21] and if I return safely to my father's home, then the LORD will certainly be my God. [22] And this memorial pillar I have set up will become a place for worshiping God, and I will present to God a tenth of everything he gives me."[7]

Jacob's angelic encounter illustrates that angels are inhabitants of two realms—Heaven and earth. They are equally at home in either place, and although we may not always be able to see them, we know they are active and carrying out God's commands.

Jacob's encounter did not persuade him to worship angels, but the Lord God, who was clearly over the angels. At Bethel, Jacob determined to serve God throughout his life, and he never wavered from that commitment.

CHAPTER THREE

MINISTERING ANGEL

TRACY MCGARVEY

When I was twenty years old, I learned I was pregnant with my second child. Problem was, I'd been taking birth control shots, so I wasn't supposed to get pregnant. One of the side effects of those birth control shots was the possibility of giving birth to a child with severe birth defects.

During my first trimester, the doctors detected a heart defect in the sonogram. They immediately scheduled me for amniocentesis—the sampling of amniotic fluid to screen for developmental abnormalities in an unborn baby. After the procedure, the staff met with me for a brief counseling session, a meeting that only heightened my fears. After being told I could give birth to a deformed infant, everyone left the room. All I could do was look out the floor-length rectangular window.

I heard a voice tell me to jump. *Just jump; your baby is going to be deformed, and you will never have a life of your own.*

But I didn't jump. With the way things were going in my personal life, I was pretty sure I would survive and end up with a bunch of broken bones.

Because the doctors wouldn't know the final test results for two weeks, I left that office convinced I had inadvertently ruined two lives—mine and my unborn child's.

One day, my mother-in-law invited me to a prayer gathering at her friend's house. As I walked toward the door, I saw children with special needs sitting on the porch. Some were wearing oxygen masks, some were in wheelchairs, some of them had deformed limbs. What was my mother-in-law thinking, inviting me to a house like that?

Then I heard that same voice in my head: *Your child is going to be just like these children.*

I blocked the voice from my head and went into the home, my footsteps as heavy as my heart. After the meeting started, our hostess looked at me. "Do you want your baby to be healed?"

"Yes! Of course!"

"Do you want to be saved?"

"Yes!" I was desperate and would do whatever I had to do to deliver a healthy baby. If that meant surrendering my life to Jesus, I'd do it. I'd certainly made a mess of things on my own.

When several intercessors began to pray, I felt as though I was growing lighter by the moment. During that prayer time, I received Jesus as my Lord and Savior, and the Holy Spirit came to live in me. I went into that house as a spiritually dead woman and came out as a new creature in Christ Jesus, alive!

The change in me was so evident people noticed it right away. My anger problem and my near-constant use of profanity disappeared. I felt a love for people I never felt before. The world looked and felt like a different place because I saw it with new eyes and felt it with a new heart.

After that supernatural experience, I felt I could conquer anything with God. At that point, I knew, even if God did not heal my baby, I was going to serve Him anyway.

The results from the amniocentesis were negative for Down syndrome. However, the doctors continued to insist the baby would probably have a defective heart or clubbed foot, so they would need a specialist on call when I delivered my child.

My mother—who had also been praying for my baby—and I decided we would not tell other family members what the doctors said about my unborn child. But my husband had been chatting with his cousin about the potential diagnosis. He told me I needed to abort the baby, and his cousin agreed.

I didn't agree, so as I waited for my child to be born, I endured many days of building my faith. I read all the healing scriptures I could find in the Bible. Almost every hour of the day, I meditated on the healing word of God. I had to do this because during my last few months of pregnancy I had to visit the obstetrician every two weeks. In those visits, I was surrounded by no fewer than three physicians at a time.

They didn't use these exact words, but I discovered I was a medical guinea pig. They were very interested in the effects of that birth control injection on a fetus. I'm sure they meant no harm, but often they'd talk about the potential abnormalities my baby could have, and I had to lie there and listen to all those negative possibilities. I never rebuked the doctors while in their presence, but as soon as they left, I rebuked every negative word spoken into that examination room. I was determined no one would shake my confidence in Christ Jesus.

Finally, I went into labor. My doctors were ready, the special-ists were on call, and my Christian friends were praying. And when my daughter Lace was born, the only unusual condition she had was *duodenal atresia*, a situation in which the first part of the small bowel is closed and cannot allow the passage of stomach contents. The treatment is surgery.

My baby got the help she needed, and the surgery was successful. The Lord strengthened me during her hospitalization and helped me mature in the faith.

The doctors discharged Lace a month early when her nasogastric tube mysteriously came out and she was able to go twenty-four hours without vomiting. I was able to take my baby home.

I was delighted to have my daughter home with me, but I was not completely relaxed. She seemed so small and fragile. I prayed over her and asked the Lord to continue to keep her safe, but aren't all new parents a little nervous? I began to worry that something would happen while she slept—she had to sleep in an inclined position to prevent her from choking or inhaling anything she might spit up. For those first few nights, I got up every hour to check on her.

One night as I woke to examine her, I caught my breath—next to her bassinet, I saw a white glowing image, something that appeared to be a heavenly creature. As I slowly lifted my head, I saw a face, but the light was so bright I could not see details. I did not see any wings, but that didn't matter. The heavenly being did not speak, but the presence of God flooded the room, and the peace of God washed over me. I never worried again. At that moment, I knew the Lord was showing me He was watching over my baby girl.

Today, Lace is a mother to two healthy children of her own: a son, Maximus, and a daughter, Scarlette. She has accepted Jesus Christ as her Lord and Savior and has led many others to know him personally. She prays for the sick, and they are healed, believers and nonbelievers alike.

Ever since the day I met Jesus—a conviction reinforced by the sight of that angel next to my baby's bassinette—I know I do not need to worry about the future. Everything that happens to me is by God's design, and He will always keep me in the center of His hand.

Tracy McGarvey currently resides in Georgia with her husband, Owen. Together, they have six daughters ranging from nineteen to thirty years old. Tracy has a bachelor of science degree in nursing and currently works in psychiatry. She has also authored a book, *But God, He's My Husband Uncensored*. One day, she plans to pursue a master's degree in nursing and open a practice as an advanced registered nurse practitioner.

ANGEL GLIMPSES

Do Angels Have Wings?

Some angels do have wings. At least the ones Isaiah saw in his vision had wings (Is. 6:2). In fact, the seraphim each had three pairs of wings. One pair covered each angel's face, one pair the feet, and with the third pair, each angel flew (6:2). The cherubim Ezekiel saw had four wings each (Ezek. 1:11). The fact the angel Gabriel went to Daniel "in swift flight" (Dan. 9:21, NIV) suggests Gabriel has wings. The same is true of an angel whom the apostle John saw "flying in mid-air" (Rev. 14:6, NIV).

Does this mean all angels have wings? Not necessarily, although they may have. Whether all angels have or do not have wings, they can and do carry out God's bidding swiftly. They are never late in fulfilling an assignment.[8]

CHAPTER FOUR

A DREAM COME TRUE

BRETT DEWEY

When I was forty years old, I moved back home to California. A visit to the old church parking lot sat atop my to-do list. Perhaps showing my kids the two-story, pale blue house where I grew up or taking them for a slice at Tony's Pizza would have been a better idea. Those ordinary stops would show them that I, too, have a history. Even dads need to be humanized. But I had a date with the church blacktop.

Much had changed over my twenty years away. Calvary Community Church used to meet in a warehouse along a road dissecting an industrial park. The building was no longer a church, but an indoor playground. Fun became the new product manufactured there. Calvary built a new facility a mile away and continued to grow and expand its ministries.

I had changed, too. I went from single to married and a father of four daughters. I graduated from college and seminary and endured doctoral studies. I lived in places throughout southern California, then moved to Waco, Texas, and Wichita, Kansas. Then I came home again.

After I parked, I found the spot and stood on the blacktop without fear. That was new. I pivoted in the center of the asphalt. Summer had erupted in a sticky feeling underfoot. The lot shimmered with heat and smelled like a melted tire. I spun in quarter turns, remembering. The acrobatic walks across the top of the high cinder block wall. Where I had been standing when the church member snatched the loaf of bread from my hands. Remembering friends circled in prayer. Remembering a moment both dreadful and divine.

THE WAREHOUSE

As a kid, I thought worshiping in a warehouse church was radical. Christian fellowship in an industrial park imparted an odd prestige in my younger mind. A casual California vibe pushed aside old-school formalities. "Sunday best" meant designer flip-flops. Theater seating replaced pews. The accountability of the offering plate gave way to back-of-the-room "love boxes" available for discreet giving. Worship buzzed with praise, and prayers rolled in off-the-cuff style.

I overheard my best friend's mom say Calvary was the largest Catholic church in town. She used to attend St. Julie Catholic Church but recognized a lot of people despite being new to Calvary. We joined around the same time. Every summer, her son David and I rode our bikes to the St. Julie's carnival where, with a few strategically placed ping-pong balls, we would win a new set of pet goldfish. After taking in the sights, we biked home with our prizes sloshing inside twist-tied baggies.

In my younger years, my world was limited to whatever I saw in my travels on two wheels, which meant Catholicism was priests with collars, carnivals, and my goldfish, Mo, Larry, and Curly. Little did those poor fish know having me as a caretaker would be terminal. When they died, I tied two sticks together, etched a the figure of Jesus into the vertical twig, and buried them in the backyard. I tried my best to provide a Catholic funeral.

Calvary intrigued me in my youth. I didn't know a Catholic from a Protestant in those days; I only knew Calvary's pastor wore khakis, and I never got a chance to win a goldfish at church. The annual harvest festival was as close to a carnival as we would ever get; it was a Halloween party without the fun of candy and scary costumes. Who wanted to bob for apples when you could dress as a mummy and go to the house that gave away full-size candy bars? Not me. But still, Calvary was the first church I considered home.

I didn't know what Calvary was. It was not Catholic, despite what I overheard from David's mom. It also was not Baptist. I was born Baptist. To my childish mind, that meant singing hymns about Jesus's blood accompanied by an organ. Calvary did not have an organ. But it had thousands of people worshiping God, many of whom were transplants from other ways of being Christian.

In moments of surprise and joy, I would stumble into conversations with the small pockets of people who spoke in tongues, experienced healing, or even waged spiritual battle against Satan. My friend Rick's dad was delivered from Satanism, and hearing his stories thrilled me.

Christians of all stripes worshiped together at Calvary. I liked that. Except for the one time when one of the former Catholics scolded me in the church parking lot for eating the leftover communion bread. I stumbled unaware upon some theological debate I didn't understand, but I had all the facts I needed. The loaf was Hawaiian bread, and I was hungry.

Outside the sanctuary walls, the church kept unique company. I spied on the neighbors after service as I placed foot in front of foot, arms outstretched, edging my way across the cinder block wall that divided the properties. Manufacturers, insurance agencies, car repair shops, and other businesses surrounded us. Calvary snatched up adjacent buildings as we grew or our neighbors moved out.

I came to faith at Calvary Community Church and was pleased, I discovered later, with the denominational diversity of its members. So much difference, so little fighting.

As I matured through the years, and even when I failed, that warehouse and the people inside provided some of the happiest moments of my life. Weekdays in the industrial park were for commerce, but weekends were for the Lord.

THE DREAM

One evening, I was getting ready for bed when I heard a creaking outside my bedroom door. It was probably my brother. Did I need to be on my guard? We liked to prank each other. Our classic trick was to pick the bathroom lock when the other was taking a hot shower. The one with the bucket would creep in, stand on the toilet, and dump ice water on the unsuspecting brother. Prank paranoia was a thing.

I turned toward the door. It flew open.

The man who stood there was not my brother. Instead, I saw a soiled brown coat. Menacing eyes. And a knife. A long slender blade held at the ready.

A raspy voice bellowed from the disheveled man. "I'm going to kill you!"

I screamed and charged. I do not know how I did it, but I shoved him aside and bounded down the stairs. I flung open the front doors and ran for my life. I glanced back at the pale blue house to see if I got away.

Then I woke up.

That nightmare replayed in the theater of my mind all summer after my college graduation. The core elements were always the same. An unkempt man in a brown coat threatened to murder me with a knife. Terrified, I ran for my life. Every night.

At first, I thought nothing of it. But as summer went on, the nightmare began to exhaust me.

I wondered if my subconscious was playing tricks on me. I was headed for seminary, so perhaps this nightmare was a sign of some inner angst or uncertainty.

Or maybe my imagination ripped events from the headlines and fashioned them into night terrors. The summer of 1994 was full of drama, thanks to the O.J. Simpson murder case. Iconic images connected with that story still resonate. The white Bronco, O.J. trying on the bloody glove that did not fit. And the murder weapon—a slender stiletto knife. All the elements were there—violence, brown coat, knife. Perhaps I had woven those tales of death into a recurring dream.

Then the nightmare stopped. For a full week, I slept in peace. No more threats. No man in a brown coat. No knife.

During that week, I served as a summer Christian camp counselor. I enjoyed the fellowship, but even more, I enjoyed the respite from nightly dread.

When we returned from camp and reunited all the kids with their waiting parents, the camp staff circled in the church parking lot for a final prayer. My friend Rick led us. I always enjoyed his prayers. He had a spiritual insight I envied. His dad was a spiritual warrior, and it was apparent to the younger generation his son also had gifts.

As Rick prayed, recounting our common thanks for a great week at camp, he suddenly stopped talking. The pause was awkward. When he finally spoke again, he thanked God for the circle of angels around us, protecting us from evil. God's angels were ministering to us, he said, providing a hedge of spiritual protection.

I sneaked a peak and saw nothing.

We said our unison "Amen," and I walked straight over to Rick.

"What was that about?"

He hesitated but only a second. "While I was praying, I saw a homeless-looking man in a brown coat standing behind you and stabbing you in the back."

My blood ran cold as Rick went on to tell me that when he paused during the prayer, he was asking God's angels to encamp around us.

My blood was still chilly. I said as much.

"But," Rick said, "God's angels circled us and protected us."

I then recounted my recurring nightmare to Rick. The details matched. He saw what I had been dreaming. We stood there, dumbfounded. Then I asked the most important question: "What am I supposed to do with this, Rick?"

If he could see visions of angels, I expected him to have an answer.

His response was not helpful. "I don't know," he said. Then he hazarded a guess. "Maybe God is preparing you for something."

For what? Rick didn't know, and neither did I.

ST. JIMMY AND SANDWICHES

Everything is oversized in Texas, where I attended graduate school—including my grumbling about the weather. The summer miracle of coastal California is the evening cool-down, like a refreshing cloth on your forehead when you have a fever. Texas does not have an evening miracle. After sundown, the air felt like God turned on an oven to make sure we were all well done.

The heat almost broke me. I lamented to friends back on the coast, "It's been thirty days of triple digits, and at night it stays about the same!"

Locals spoke about the temperature with country poetry. "Even Satan's hot today, boy!"

The only poetry I could muster was a complaint.

But Jimmy Dorrell's church was cool, especially on Sunday mornings in January. Not cool because it met in a warehouse. Church Under the Bridge met, well, under a bridge. Its name was not a metaphor.

On chilly Sundays, the preacher greeted the congregation gathered under the Interstate 40 overpass: "If Hell is hot, then this must be Heaven!"

Teeth-chattering chuckles followed. Cold breath poured from worshipers' mouths like subway-vent smoke. In that strange place, people gathered under the bridge like good-hearted Christian trolls. They were the rich and poor, people of all colors, educated at schools or by hard knocks. They were the house-blessed and homeless. Whoever they were, they were together. That was, and is, Church Under the Bridge. A cool idea. Jimmy is not a Catholic, but I immediately thought him a saint.

Church Under the Bridge was a people, not a building. From its beginning, they worked to better the lives of the poor in Waco, a city where nearly one in three people lived below the poverty level. There was a lot of work to do, especially to help those who suffered the indignities of homelessness.

But Jimmy Dorrell had an additional calling, not only to get the rich to support the poor but to understand them. So once a year, he led "poverty simulations" where the rich paid fifty dollars for the opportunity to be poor for a weekend. Participants lived on the streets, scavenged for meals, and had to find their way for forty-eight hours. The situation was often cold, dangerous, and life-changing.

Jimmy longed to see wealthy Christians understand that the poor need more than soup kitchens and clothes closets. They need relationships. The wealthy are no different, especially those who suffer the loneliness of our age. Saint Jimmy and his friends were theological mad scientists. And on Sunday mornings, their glorious experiment broke out into worship.

When I said I met Jimmy Dorrell, I bent the truth. We've never met face to face. My buddy Dale knew Jimmy and told me all about him. He invited me to worship under the interstate, but I always refused. The fact was, I was too afraid to visit. Thoughts of worshipping with the homeless and outcasts made me sweat like it was Texas in July. The fear stemmed from that recurring dream and the powerful experience in the Calvary Community parking lot, an ordeal still rippling through my life.

Was a homeless man out there waiting for me? I didn't want to find out.

Another decade passed, my family grew, and God blessed us with a healthy and joyful church family. I was pastor at Hope Mennonite Church in Wichita, Kansas, where commitments to peacemaking and sandwich-making were core values. Hope participated in Sandwich Saturdays, a Wichita-area church ministry run through St. John's Episcopal Church. Once a month, we made hundreds of brown-bag lunches, drove into the shadows of downtown high rises, and hand delivered the lunches to the homeless population.

It was a humble ministry. The causes of homelessness are complex and so are its solutions. Ham sandwiches and potato chips do not solve problems, but the ministry helps the destitute with food and relationships. It gets members of area churches face-to-face with people in need. Jimmy taught me that was important.

Even more, St. John's ministry does not simply serve food, it serves stories. A lending library empowers the homeless, often families with children, to feed their minds and spirits. Seeing those folks with books helped me see them in a new way—fully human.

Still, I feared dirty and potentially dangerous men, not because I ever met one but because of what happened years earlier in the church parking lot. But perhaps the strangest thing of all was that even that event was an answer to prayer.

For years, you see, I prayed to experience God in a mystical way. Tales of the supernatural fascinated me all the way back to those eye-opening stories I heard as a kid at Calvary. As a teen-ager, I prayed for the gift of tongues. I would turn off the radio on the way home from youth group. As I drove, I would open my mouth and try to almost vomit out spiritual utterances. It never worked.

The year before angels ministered to me in that parking lot, I was circled in prayer with friends home from college for Christ-mas break. My newly minted friend D.C. was there sporting a knee brace. A new Christian himself, he tore his ACL on a recent cross-country team run.

About a dozen friends crowded into a condo living room and prayed. Some of us held hands. But another friend placed her hand on D.C.'s knee as we petitioned God. Solemn voices spoke softly. Earnestness dripped from our teenage hearts.

That's why we were all surprised when D.C. screamed. We all looked at this new Christian and thought, *In case you didn't know, you aren't supposed to scream during prayer.*

Turns out, the hand on his knee got red hot, he testified, and the heat radiated through his knee. He was healed.

He took off his brace and bent his knee. The swelling was gone. The pain was no more. An honest-to-God miracle.

And my first thought was, *Why can't that happen to me?* I wanted the healing without the torn ligament. I should have been thankful for D.C. and left it at that.

My teenage prayers were mostly of the bargain variety. Like when I asked God to get me a date with Gina Luccirello, and in return, I would stop cussing. I got the date, but my language did not improve. My assumption was God only gave you what you asked for if you offered something in return. I weirdly assumed, after God gave His son for the sake of the world, for some reason He turned stingy. Prayer required bargains.

Then I read Mark 10. Jesus asked the blind man, "What do you want me to do for you?" Jesus did not ask him to make a deal. He wanted to know the desire of the man's heart.

I learned that was true for me, too. I stopped making bargains with God, although I continued to pray I would experience the reality of God in a powerful way.

I believe the ministering of God's angels in that church parking lot was an answer to that prayer. It took two decades to see the ministering angels in that story because I'd been so blinded by my fear of death. But that's my fault.

GAZE ON CHRIST

I was thirty-nine years old when my friend Corey died of brain cancer. His death stung. He was a creative and mechanical genius. He designed motorcycles for a living and in his spare time created "tot rods," baby strollers that looked like souped-up street cars. He adored his wife and son. He loved Jesus deeply. Our friendship was built on that. His loss exposed my deep fear of death.

To help me cope, I read a book by Dale Aukerman titled *Hope Beyond Healing: A Cancer Journal.* Dale was a pastor, farmer, and peace activist and chronicled his battle with cancer through daily diary entries. After he and his wife received bad news from the doctor near the end of his life, Ruth said, "The devil wants us to stare at death, but we are to gaze at Christ."

That line changed everything for me.

The devil wants us to stare at death. The devil wanted me to stare at the man in the brown coat and freeze in fear every time I saw a homeless man.

But we are to gaze at Christ. We are to gaze at His ministering angels. We are to see God's loving kindness and trust His goodness.

I see that now. I am embarrassed it took me so long to understand, but not as embarrassed as I would be had I never figured it out.

God did not prepare me to spend twenty years fearing men in brown coats. He prepared me to love Catholics, Baptists, non-denominationals, and non-Christians. God called me to love house-dwellers and the houseless, to love all people of all kinds made by the all-loving God.

Standing on that sticky asphalt in the California parking lot, I remembered what I had learned and looked forward to what I would learn in the future. I will move ahead and not be afraid because my gaze is on—and my trust is in—Christ alone.

Brett Dewey is a high school teacher, pastor, and expedition leader on the adventure of life's big questions. For more than thirty years, he has served as an ambassador for the Kingdom of God, a job he plans to keep forever. He lives near Los Angeles, California, with his wife Esther and their four daughters.

ANGEL GLIMPSES

An old minister worked into the night on a sermon for his small congregation. His unsympathetic wife chided him for spending so much time on a message that so few will appreciate. To this the minister replied: "You forget, my dear, how large my audience will be!"

If angels are looking, nothing on earth done for Christ is trivial.[9]

CHAPTER FIVE

ANGEL IN MY LIVING ROOM

PEGGY PATRICK MEDBERRY

The smooth brown pebble felt cold in my hand. It had a strange symbol, like a broken C, carved into it. I looked for the interpretation in a little leather-bound book. *Darkness. Mysterious beginning.*

I placed the rune carefully on my dining room table next to its little drawstring burlap bag. I noticed another paragraph. *Make sure you have protected the area before you lay out the stones.* The little book that came with the runes listed several needed items. Oops. I probably should have read the directions first.

I went to the kitchen to get the box of Morton's Salt. Protection from what?

I checked on my two-year-old sleeping safely in the next room. She would be napping for at least two hours. That gave me thirty minutes to set up before the ritual was to begin. I was going to finally get my life back. At least that's what the book I got at the grocery store said.

I never imagined life as a stay-at-home mom. In fact, the phrase *stay-at-home mom* wasn't even a term in 1972. Most women with little children were expected to stay home with their children until they were in school. But that was never supposed to be me because I always thought I'd be a star.

I should be in New York right now.

I looked at my beautiful daughter. She was sound asleep. Her blonde hair curled on her cheek as she cuddled her favorite red and white bear.

I shifted my gaze and stared vacantly out the window at a palm tree dancing in the afternoon breeze. I imagined myself in a sleek black turtleneck and jeans, briskly leaving my tiny apartment and catching the subway to a cavernous theater somewhere in the city. I could hear people rehearsing their lines and smell the musty wood floors and leather seats. It would be cool in New York now—maybe the trees would be turning brilliant colors.

A palm frond scratched at the window, dissolving my daydream.

I went back to the dining room where my little stones waited for me. Runes. An ancient alphabet created by Vikings and later used to create magic spells. The little bag of carved rocks was attached to a faux leather book that promised success, wealth, and anything you could desire. You just had to call on the spirits of the runes to come help you.

I picked up the box of salt and began to pour it on the carpet in a large circle. The salt was to keep the entities from escaping the circle and getting into the rest of the house. That was why I waited for Anna to be asleep and not in the dining room. The book told me I would be dealing with powerful forces and to take great care in my preparation for the divination ritual. Losing control of them could be dangerous.

The book described all sorts of stories of people who used the power of the runes. Great kings ruled and won wars with these forces but lost their kingdoms when they stopped using them.

Even the Nazis were thought to have acquired their power from the occult and messages they received from the runes.

I figured those were only entertaining stories someone exaggerated to sell rocks with little scratches on them. How dangerous could runes be? At least I would be entertained. Boredom had become my primary pastime since moving to Florida.

If only my professors could see me now. I majored in theater in college, and for four years, I was their "star." All my teachers were sure I had a shot at regional theater or even Broadway. I was even selected to study in England with a famous playwright for a summer semester. Everyone assumed that after school I would go to New York and try my luck on the legitimate stage.

I pulled out a sort of square stone and placed it on the table. This one had a double X. Hmmm. *Fertility*. How ironic. How perfect.

My New York dream came crashing down the spring of my sophomore year. My on-again, off-again boyfriend, Joey, and I discovered we were going to be parents. After three months of missed periods and wrenching morning sickness, I finally admitted it was true. I was planning to break up with him. But not knowing what to do, Joey and I secretly eloped over a weekend. Because I was in the middle of a play and living at home, we decided to not tell my parents we got married, much less that I was pregnant, until school was out. So, we kept up the charade for six more weeks.

I remember feeling like I was walking under water during those weeks. Joey and I had been in a turbulent relationship since my freshman year. He saw me in a play and thought I was beautiful and talented. He pursued me with flowers and gifts. But once we started going out, he became jealous of everyone and everything. At the time, that sort of attention was flattering—that someone could love me so much he wanted me all to himself.

What I didn't realize was how suffocating life could become with a man who needed to control me completely.

You knew, Joey! You knew theater was my dream, my life.

I arranged the two runes according to the diagram in the book.

Once a child came into the equation, everything changed. Peggy wasn't going to be an actress. She was going to be a mother.

My interpretation of what a mother looked like came from my own mom. My mother was raised to be a Southern Belle. She majored in home economics and married my war-hero father. She planned to cook, garden, and interior-decorate her life into the sunset.

But the culture was changing. The Sixties. Women's liberation. Being a homemaker was looked down on. Women were supposed to have a job. Only women who were untalented and dumb stayed home. If you had a brain, you were supposed to use it and become something.

At least that was the message my mother got, and she felt trapped with four children in our small university town. She was desperately unhappy. I saw her misery and swore I would never end up in her situation.

Many years later, she and I talked about how she was caught in that tragic cultural riptide. The lie fomented by that movement wasn't that women shouldn't have careers if they wanted them, it was that being a mother was not an important and fulfilling job. My mother and I were both a product of the times.

I felt in the bag for another stone. This one looked like a J. *Harvest. Growth. Fruitfulness.*

Growing progressively larger with child as I attended college classes was embarrassing. But, I kept up my studies during the fall semester and took my finals early, knowing the baby was due in

December. On December fifth, my beautiful baby daughter Anna came into the world.

Of course, I fell immediately in love with her. When I gazed at her huge blue eyes and porcelain skin, my heart melted. I could do this. I could be a mother.

The rest of college passed in a blur. Although hectic, Joey and I had fun being a young couple with a baby. We worked out our schedules so we could trade off watching her. My mother helped, too.

By that spring I was back on the stage, starring in *Oliver.* I did summer stock again that summer. Anna played in a playpen just off stage when we rehearsed. Joey watched her at night when I was performing. By the end of my senior year, I became adept at balancing motherhood, school, and acting.

We talked about how we would go to New York after graduation, I would pursue acting, and Joey would get a wonderful job. Life seemed possible. Then Joey got a great job offer in Florida, and they wanted him immediately.

New York would have to wait. Even though I was already cast in the theater company for the summer, Joey insisted I come with him instead of waiting to follow at the end of the repertory season. By June, I found myself in the middle of hot, muggy, buggy Florida with a teething toddler.

I drew the next stone and placed it on the table. It looked like a capital I. *Ice. Frozen.*

Frozen in time. My whole career, everything came to a halt. Once the shock of losing my dream wore off, I discovered boredom and depression. I was thousands of miles away from my mother in a completely alien environment. Joey spent all day at work. I stayed at home and washed diapers and hung them to dry on our balcony. My days became a recurring drudge of watching television while Anna played. Feeding her. Giving her a nap.

Watching more television. Cleaning the house and making sure dinner was ready when Joey got home.

The stones were telling my story. I pulled out the next one. This time it looked like a little bow tie. *Daylight. Dawn.* Oh, yes, I had seen a glimmer of hope.

One day while grocery shopping, I saw a flyer for a community theater in the area. They were having tryouts. My heart leaped.

At first, Joey said no; he didn't want me gone at night. We fought bitterly. I told him he could at least let me try out to see if I got cast in something. I finally wore him down, and a couple of weeks later, I was cast as the breezy love interest in *Flowers for Algernon.*

Oh, how I loved being up on the stage again, surrounded by people who told me I was talented and beautiful. I could disappear into a role and not be me for a few hours a couple of times a week.

But the better I felt, the angrier Joey became. He hated that I was acting again. He said acting was a stupid, frivolous pastime. I reminded him he fell in love with me because of my acting. He said things were different now—it was time for me to grow up and be a mother. He constantly harped on my housekeeping and criticized my weight. I started believing him.

Despite my guilt over being a bad wife and mother and for wanting to continue acting, I kept at it. The play was a success. I got great reviews. I became the talented "newcomer to the area theater scene."

Only a few more stones to place. The next one was a lopsided X with a line through it. *Caution. Destructive forces.*

A cold shiver went through me. This game was supposed to be fun. Hopefully, the salt would protect me.

Why was I even fooling around with this stuff? I felt like I was living a double life. By day, a boring, depressed housewife. By night, a glamorous actress.

I knew the truth. I was just a housewife. I had ruined my life, and being "just a housewife" was my lovely parting gift.

Our constant fighting killed the few feelings I ever had for Joey. I wasn't ever in love with him. I planned to break up with him before we found out I was pregnant. So I made the best of a bad situation. My marriage started in a relationship already on a downward spiral. But I tried desperately to pretend we were okay. I was an actress, after all.

To avoid Joey's constant criticism, I frantically tried to keep the house picked up. I struggled to lose the last few pounds of baby weight. I lived in fear he would say I couldn't act anymore. I made sure Anna was fed and bathed and in bed by the time I left for rehearsal. I raced back to the house after the two hours were over. I was not in New York, but this would do.

Outside, the wind picked up and made a tree scrape against the wall. The room was feeling a little chilly. I checked the thermostat, but the temperature was sitting at 72.

Feeling a bit nervous, I got up and sprinkled more salt around the table. I was missing my afternoon soap operas for this. I spent $5 on this silliness, so I might as well get my money's worth.

I'd found the stones and the book at the grocery store a few days earlier. The day was a real scorcher when I ventured out on my weekly shopping trip. I circled the parking lot for thirty minutes, trying to find a parking space. Anna played on the seat next to me while I searched the lot in my shuddering Volkswagen Beetle. We were relieved when we could finally get out of the car.

I pulled my waist-length ponytail up in a bun. Sweat dripped down the back of my halter top as I stepped into the bright sunlight filtering through big puffy clouds.

"Look Anna, a butterfly!" I pointed to a fluffy cloud with wispy wings.

"Buhfwy!" Anna laughed as she looked at the sky. *Butterfly* was her first clear word when she was three months old. She had a little soft book I showed her every night. She would point to the butterfly and squeal with delight. "Buhfwy!"

"Here's a cookie." I fished an animal cracker out of my Indian print bag and handed it to her as I hoisted her onto my hip. Hopefully, the cookie would hold her attention during my quick trip inside the store. Happily, I found a cart to put her in. Three wheels wobbled and one was completely frozen. But judging from the conditions of the parking lot, the store was packed and this might be my only choice.

"Okay. Let's see what we need to get . . ." By that time, Anna had turned the cookie into a soggy mess. Oh well.

I dug a crumpled list out of my purse. "Okay, we need more cloth diapers. We need detergent, fabric softener, toilet paper." I would also pick up a case of baby food and more teething biscuits.

The air conditioning blew delicious, cool air as we moved through the store. I paused at the jewelry counter and looked at the pretty necklaces and earrings. Oh, to feel pretty and glamorous. And happy. When did happiness leave me?

"Hey, Peggy!" My neighbor, Paula, waved at me from the baby food aisle. She had her two boys in tow. Paula was the first friend I had made when I moved to Florida. Her apartment was across the courtyard from mine, and we met at the pool.

"Hi, Paula—picking up baby stuff."

"Me, too. I've got two of these guys to keep up with. They are eating machines." She laughed as she grabbed her four-year-old's hand away from a tower of cans. Her eight-month-old cooed in the cart.

I sighed. "You're a natural at this. I wish I could breeze through motherhood like you do."

Everything about Paula said *born to be a mom*. Her kids were happy, her house was clean, her husband was nice. I even envied her houseplants.

"Really? I wish I could be a glamorous star like you!"

I laughed. "Hardly a star. And it's only community theater."

"The reviews say you are a fresh newcomer to St. Petersburg's theater scene."

"I am so glad you are my friend, Paula. You're probably the only person in town who even read that review."

"Gotta get in line—but let's take the kids out by the pool tomorrow, okay?"

She breezed off toward the front of the store.

A few cases of baby food later, I was ready to check out. Had it not been for the old couple paying for their purchases with rolled-up quarters and the lady in front of me with a wallet of coupons, I might not have noticed the book.

Anna was becoming cranky. As I waited, my eyes wandered to the wire rack filled with paperbacks. *Find Your Soulmate. Catch Him With White Magic.* No interest there.

Mystical Gardens of Scotland—What's Their Secret? The pictures of pumpkin-sized tomatoes intrigued me. I tossed the booklet into my cart.

Next to it was a slim book with a little bundle of rocks tied to it. *The Book of Runes.* Curious, I picked it up and looked at the back. *How to have the happy, fulfilled life of your dreams . . .* The book promised money, power, success, and romance—all by using the magic of the runes. That certainly sounded like a good idea.

I placed the book on the conveyor belt and smiled at the young cashier. She rang up my purchases, then I handed her my driver's license as I wrote out a check.

"Wow! You're Peggy Patrick!"

I lifted a brow. "Yes."

"I saw you in that play! You were great!"

I blushed. She was absolutely the first person who ever recognized me from a role I played on stage.

"You were so funny! I go to the Little Theater all the time."

"Thank—thank you," I stammered. "I—uh—I'm new in town. I hope to do more."

"Oh, I'm sure you will! It's exciting to have a celebrity come through my checkout." She loaded my bags into my cart. Your baby is *so* cute, too!"

I looked at Anna. She was covered in soggy animal cookie. "Well, thank you so much. I'm not really a celeb —"

The check-out girl had turned to the next customer.

I pushed the cart into the stultifying heat, but not before I caught a glimpse of my reflection in the glass doors. My ponytail-bun had mostly come undone. Long wet strands of hair were plastered to my neck. My jean cutoffs were tattered, and I had major baby food and coffee stains on my top. No makeup. Hardly a glamorous actress.

I made a mental note: *Dress a bit better the next time you dash out for groceries.*

My dining room seemed to grow darker despite the bright afternoon light that usually beamed through the window. Probably a cloud over the sun. But I felt my stomach twist as I sat to study the book for more directions. It said I needed a goblet of water.

I went into the kitchen to fill one of the Waterford crystal goblets we got as a wedding gift. This was supposed to be another protection from the spirits. Apparently, spirits don't like water, either.

I felt uneasy as I filled the glass. I looked out the kitchen window and saw my two neighbors, Paula and Ellen, by the pool.

The pool was a welcome oasis in the hot Florida sun. Yesterday I sat in the baby pool with Anna, splashing and laughing, while Paula watched Ben and Danny play in the shallow end of the adult pool. Another neighbor, Ellen, wandered out to join us.

Ellen had stunning movie-star looks—long black hair and beautiful Polynesian features. Her husband sold Cadillacs, and I thought he was too slick by half. He was the kind of guy who leered at every female in the room, and Ellen was well aware of his roaming eye.

Paula looked up from her lounge chair as Ellen came over. "How's it going in Ellen-land?"

"Howie came in at 2:00 a.m." Ellen plopped down and began applying suntan lotion on her perfect legs.

I gave Anna a floaty duck to play with. "Where was he?"

"Oh—with friends, supposedly talking about sports." Ellen rolled her eyes.

"What do *you* think?" Paula asked cautiously.

"I don't know. I want to believe him." Ellen leaned back in her chair. "But I don't."

We sat in silence. Only the sound of the kids laughing and splashing helped cover the awkwardness.

"Don't feel sorry for me." Ellen turned over on her stomach. She seemed entirely too calm. "I've planned it all out."

"What? Killing him?" I asked.

"Oh, heck no." Ellen looked up at me. "I've planned how much money I'm going to get in the divorce settlement. I just need him to buy me a house first."

"Does he have any idea you suspect?"

"He'd have to be pretty stupid not to. I don't think he cares."

"You'd actually get a divorce?" In 1972, divorces weren't all that common. "What would your parents say?"

I shuddered at the thought. Unhappy as I was, the idea of having to tell my parents I wanted a divorce was something I'd never be able to do. If your marriage is unhappy, too bad. You made your bed, now lie in it. Also, I didn't have a good reason to consider such a thing. Joey was controlling, mean, jealous, and occasionally violent, but he paid the bills. I didn't think he was unfaithful.

Ellen laughed as she piled her gorgeous hair up in a loose bun. "My parents would help me pay for the attorneys. They hate Howie. And it's not like I can't find another man to support me. I may have even already found one." She smiled slyly.

I managed to conceal my shock. Not because she was thinking about other men—I was tempted to look around at the cute guys at rehearsals—but by her brazen admission that she would consider infidelity.

Ellen stretched out her perfect body on the lounge chair. "How's the play going?"

"Oh, it's great. We open in a couple of weeks."

"How's Joey putting up with it?"

I made a face. I had told them my sad story many times.

"He should support you in what you are doing." Paula chimed in.

"He thinks I should be home being a mom."

Ellen undid the back of her bikini to avoid a tan line. "Hello—it's a new day! Women are rising up. No one stays home anymore unless you're wealthy or you're Paula."

"I love being home." Paula laughed. "I'm thrilled I don't have to work."

"I'll take being wealthy—along with a cute pool boy." Ellen smiled. "But Peggy, you have real talent. You should be doing something with it. You shouldn't have to ask permission to breathe. I think you should dump Joey and run off to New York."

"What about Anna?" I brushed my daughter's beautiful golden hair out of her eyes. I tried not to show how much the idea of running away appealed to me. But that would take courage. Something I didn't have.

"Take her with you. There are babysitters in New York. I love New York. I'd be there now if Howie weren't making so much money down here in this hell hole."

"It sounds like you have fallen out of love with Howie." I knew the feeling.

"I don't know. I kind of like him, when he's not being a jerk. What I like is the money he makes, and he knows it. But I've never had a dream like you have. Except maybe about a really nice house."

Ellen turned over on her back and closed her eyes. She would have died had she known I was using her as my character study for my role of Estelle.

In my small-town mindset, people met, fell in love, and married. And even if the marriage was troubled, they put up with each other—forever.

At least that seemed to be my parents' formula. They fought all the time. My parents did love each other; they just had different interests. My dad was a bookish introvert, and my mother wanted to throw parties and go out dancing. Opposites attract.

My situation didn't fit any of these. Even though he didn't show it, I guessed that Joey loved me. Or had at one point. He was certainly jealous enough. And I was becoming fearful of his violent rages. He never hit me or anything. But he broke things and would storm off for hours at a time, and it could be for the slightest thing. I really didn't have the luxury of saying, "No, not tonight." That would put him in a real rage. His fury was frightening, and it seemed to have gotten worse. He knew how much I wanted to act, and he used it as a bargaining tool.

The water from the faucet overflowed the goblet and poured onto my hand. I needed to snap out of it and finish this silly ritual. I grabbed a hand towel to wipe up the water.

I carefully placed the goblet on the table where the book said it should be. The room was now icy cold. I stared at my dining room table with the runes laid out. A candle. I needed a candle. I searched for one in the hutch. Can't cast a spell without a candle. I found a green taper in the drawer. Green to fight the strife in the house. It would take a lot more than a green candle to fix Joey. Like dinner last night:

Joey smirked as he finished off the mashed potatoes. "Glad to see you eating fewer carbs—maybe it'll help with the thunder thighs."

I started to say something but stopped myself. Pointless to argue. He was doing this because I had rehearsal.

"Anna had her bath before you got home, so I will be putting her down a bit early."

Joey shrugged. He didn't really care. I breathed a sigh of relief and cleared the dishes.

"Must be nice, doing nothing all day long while I work. Lounging by the pool. Then getting to play all night."

"I did five loads of laundry. And made your dinner."

"Boy, that must have been really tough." Joey looked at me. "I wouldn't mind having your day. Especially if I got to sunbathe with your friend Ellen. She doesn't have thunder thighs."

I took a deep breath and said nothing. Joey chuckled as he left his dishes on the table and wandered into the living room.

Somehow, I managed to put Anna in bed and get out the door without a complete blow-up. Every day seemed to get worse. I never told my friends the whole truth about how mean Joey was. They knew he was unsupportive. I thought about Ellen planning to leave Howie. Could I ever have the nerve? They didn't know how he really treated me. The truth was I felt like I deserved it.

I'm doing this ritual so I can be happy again. Content. If only Joey would support me in my art. If only. Now I needed matches.

Whenever I went to rehearsal, I felt like I could breathe again.

The play I was working on was *No Exit* by Jean-Paul Sartre, an existential piece about three people in Hell. I was cast as the vain, high-society woman Estelle, who ruins her life by having an affair. Her whole life is lived selfishly.

The whole idea of the play was the characters were trapped in a world of their own making, and they were doomed forever to play out their scripts of never being fulfilled. All they had was each other. And each of them was the worst possible person for the other.

I had no problem identifying with the situation.

Not that I believed in Hell. Actually, I didn't know what I believed in. I went to Sunday school as a child and colored pictures of Jonah and the whale. I also attended the church high school group, but that was about being able to meet cute boys. So, I really hadn't formulated much of a belief system. I figured there was a God of some kind, but I guessed He was much too big and nebulous to pay any attention to creatures as small and insignificant as us. As a child, I read ghost stories and fairy tales, so I assumed there might be some realm where spirits lived, so perhaps that was Heaven or something like it. But Hell? Why did we need one? I was already living in it.

Brian, the director, sat down next to me in the theater. "Some of us are going out for drinks after rehearsal. You should come with us. Could be fun." Brian was at least twenty years older than I was, and he had a bad combover. He was a television star on some short-lived series, but he wasn't a bad director.

"I have to get back to the family." I smiled nervously. He had a reputation for hitting on the younger actresses.

"We could talk a little more deeply about your character . . ."

"Maybe another time. I promised Joey I would come straight home."

Brandi and James, my fellow cast members, chimed in. "Peggy, you ought to come. Brian always picks up the tab."

Brandi was a sexy redhead. She giggled as she flirtatiously punched Brian. I couldn't tell if she actually liked Brian or just liked getting cast in his plays.

James smiled as he leaned down and whispered in my ear. "That way I would have someone to talk to." He rolled his eyes as we watched Brandi seductively pick invisible lint off Brian's shirt.

James was cute. Tall, with dark hair and stunning blue eyes. He was also recently out of college. No girlfriend. Amazingly talented actor. Absolutely my type. Oh, the temptation.

"I can't." I looked at him for a beat too long. "And I am really sorry I can't."

James smiled kindly. "There will be another opportunity. I hope."

My heart skipped a beat. I tried not to show that I hoped so, too.

As I drove home, I fought back tears. If only—if only. If only I could be more like Ellen.

Maybe the runes would give me the courage. What was left? I checked the book. Oh, incense. And a bell.

The two books I got at the store made for interesting reading. I quickly breezed through *Mystical Gardens of Scotland*. It was primarily pictures of huge vegetables and stories of fairy sightings. Apparently, a commune lived on a farm and worshipped little sprites, who, in turn, helped them grow terrific produce. There were rock spirits, flower spirits, and water spirits. And the people maintained that by praying to them, they received ancient, secret information.

I remembered my father talking about different spirits in Scotland. I always thought they were just stories, but he did tell one particularly frightening tale about the banshee that wailed when the eldest son of a clan died. Daddy told us his mother talked about hearing the banshee when her father died.

Maybe supernatural beings could exist. Why not? Something caused things to grow. Why not fairies? Or little spirits? I turned my attention to the second book, *The Book of Runes*.

According to the author, powerful runes could bring happiness into your life. Simply by arranging them in certain ways, special magical powers could be accessed. The book described people who used the runes and suddenly became millionaires and found the love of their lives.

The book suggested the best way to use the runes was to chant a special spell to call on their powers. This needed to happen at a particular time based on the phase of the moon, the date, and exact time of day. The author outlined an entire ritual that required calling on specific entities who would come help with your desires.

What would I do if an entity showed up? The book included all sorts of warnings about powerful magic and to use at my own risk. What would I be risking? If it worked, I would be wealthy, successful, and able to leave Joey. If it didn't—well, it wasn't like I would be releasing demons into the world or anything. Well, at least I hoped not.

Another shudder went up my spine. The rocks were nothing more than a game. How lucky I was the date coincided perfectly with the appropriate phase of the moon.

I pulled a little bell out of a junk drawer. This was for summoning the spirits at the right moment. I took a deep breath. I had prepared all day for this. Anna played outside a long time earlier, so she would stay asleep.

The morning was beyond-words beautiful.

"Look Anna! An angel!" I sat on the grass while Anna played in the sandbox on the playground. The air was a bit cooler than usual, and beautiful puffy clouds danced in lovely shapes across the blue sky. One of the shapes resembled an almost classical version of a huge angel with wings, long flowing hair, and robes. The sun illuminated the cloud's edges with golden light.

"Anjuh!" Anna laughed and dug with her pail and shovel.

The cloud was so ethereal. So breathtaking. I was struck with a deep and powerful appreciation.

My eyes filled with tears. *God, I wish there were an angel to help me. I need someone to guide me.* I lowered myself to the grass and gazed at the sky, resisting an urge to break into wracking sobs. *I'm sorry I messed up so badly. I am so sorry I don't love Joey.*

What would it feel like to be really loved? I thought of handsome James. But as interesting as he was, he wasn't the love I really wanted. I wanted a deeper love. A purer love. I wanted someone to love me for who I really was. Could such a love even exist?

Anna patted me on the arm with her little chubby hand. "Anjuh."

I tickled her and she ran back to the sandbox.

I wished someone could love me the way I loved Anna. How I loved her. The love I felt for my daughter was powerful and overwhelming. Fierce. But was it possible to be a mother *and* be in the theater? Other women found a way to have a career and motherhood. There had to be a way.

Fifteen minutes before the appointed time, I looked at my preparations. The runes were in place. Everything was ready. I lit the candle, then draped a knitted throw over my shoulders to counteract the icy cold in the room. The thermostat must be broken.

I picked up the book to study the incantation. The flame on the candle flickered wildly. My hands shook as I turned to the right page. *This is simply a fun pastime*, I told myself. *Nothing is going to happen. The cold is just my imagination. The flickering, just my imagination.*

Suddenly, the phone rang, and I nearly jumped out of my skin. No one ever called. Shaking, I got up to answer it in the kitchen.

A lovely female voice greeted me. "Hi! Is this Peggy Patrick?"

"Uh—yes." I didn't recognize the voice.

"My name's Donna. I read in the paper that you are going to be in the next Little Theater play."

"Yes." I was confused.

"I saw you in the last play. You were really good. The reviews were right!"

"Uh, thank you." I had never gotten a call from a fan before.

"I happen to be in the area. Can I come meet you? I can be there in five minutes!"

I glanced over at the dining room table where the runes were laid out.

"Uh, um—well, I just put the baby down—"

"Then it's a perfect time! I would love to talk more about theater and acting and how you got into it."

I hesitated. The book was clear about the importance of the timing. If I didn't do the ritual today, I would have to wait at least a month for the right phase of the moon. And maybe even longer for certain planets to be aligned. But there was something in the woman's voice that was so kind, so loving.

"Sure, why not? I'm over at Paradise Bay. Apartment 212."

"I'll be right there."

I hung up and dashed about, picking up toys from the living room floor. I swept the runes back into their little bag and tucked them and the book in a cupboard. I had barely finished straightening up when I heard a knock. *Wow, that was fast. It hasn't even been five minutes.*

I opened the door, letting the bright afternoon light flood in. "Hi! I'm Donna."

"You really were nearby." I held the door open for her. I was amazed by the stunning woman who walked into the room. Easily six-foot-four. Long luxurious dark hair. Luminous skin and eyes. She was dressed in white palazzo pants with a flowing white kimono-style top. "You are really tall," I added.

"Everyone says that. That's why I always wear flats." She laughed.

"I always wished to be tall. Do you model?"

"No. But thank you for thinking I could be one."

"Have a seat. I'll get us some tea. I have some herbal mint. Do you like honey?"

"Absolutely."

I liked her instantly. As I prepared the tea, I thought how nice it was to meet someone new.

I carried our two cups of tea to the coffee table. "So, are you interested in theater?"

"I love it, but really just to watch it. I have always loved watching talented actors bring stories to life. How long have you been acting?"

"It's been my dream for a long time. I pursued it seriously in college. Maybe someday I'll get to New York."

"Really? Why New York?"

"That's where the best professional theater is done."

"That means everyone in this area would miss out on your talent!"

"Thank you for saying that. But there are plenty of talented people in this area."

"But only one you."

I smiled. "I guess I won't feel like I've really made it unless I get a chance to see how I would do in New York."

Donna relaxed into the couch. "So, it's sort of like a competition for you?"

I never thought about it like that. Was that the reason I wanted to be New York?

"I mean, if you love the art, can't you do it here as well as anywhere?'

"I guess that's true. It certainly is what I am trying to do."

"So, you are doing *No Exit*."

"Yes, it's about being in Hell."

"I know. Read it years ago. Existentialism. Do you believe in that?"

"What—that our lives are determined by the sum total of our actions? I don't know. It's a grim philosophy. Whatever we've done in life, that's what we are. It doesn't matter what we might have believed or wished. Our actions are all that count."

Donna sighed. "No mercy or hope there. No second chances. The gavel comes down, and if you don't measure up, too bad. Hell for you."

"My life sort of feels like that right now . . ." I said quietly. I told her about my depression and feelings of being trapped.

"You think there is no exit for you?"

"I can't see one." The conversation ceased for a moment.

Donna shifted on the couch. "Do you think it's possible you might be exactly where you should be now?"

I had spent so many months lamenting my plight, that idea hadn't occurred to me.

"I believe we all have some greater purpose than is evident to us right now," Donna went on. "That it isn't an accident we are where we are." She gentled her voice. "Perhaps there are lessons to be learned. Maybe what you are going through right now will be important later."

We continued chatting and drinking tea. She was so easy to talk to. She told me she traveled a lot in her job as a consultant and was only in the area for a couple of weeks. I told her my dreams and frustrations. She seemed to be genuinely interested in what was going on in my life.

"So, what are you reading?" Donna gestured toward the books on my coffee table.

I laughed as I grabbed the book on mystical Scottish gardens. "Are you religious?"

She smiled. "I like to think of myself as more spiritual."

"Then you might like this. I got this book at the grocery store, so it must be true. It's about fairies and sprites that live in this Scottish commune and help the people there."

She leaned in. "So, it's not a fairy tale?"

"More like a real-life fairy tale. According to this book, there are spirits that can be prayed to all over the place. If you want help, you can ask them."

"How funny!" Donna sipped her tea.

"You don't think it's possible."

"Oh, I think it's possible. I just have a different viewpoint on stuff like this. As a businesswoman, I have always found that if you want something, you go to the top."

"What do you mean?"

"You believe there could be little spirits everywhere."

"The book makes a good case for them."

"You believe in the supernatural."

"Sure."

"Well, if you want something in that realm, why not go to the top of the supernatural pecking order?"

I still didn't understand.

"Instead of fooling around with some rock spirit or flower spirit. why not direct your request to the One Who created the rock and the flower in the first place? Go to God."

I nodded. She made sense.

"Do you believe in God? You believe in spirits, so you would have to believe in God."

"I guess so. I just imagined God as some large, impersonal force that makes things grow. Isn't God or the universe or whatever too big to deal with people and their dumb requests?"

"He has all the time in the world. He's eternal." She narrowed her gaze and held me in an intense look. "Look at the world around you, the beauty, the creation, the order—everything. God created it all, down to the last detail. If He cares about the tiniest flower, why wouldn't He care about you?"

"But what about all these rock fairies?"

"What about them? They can hang out with rocks or mushrooms or whatever. But God is in charge of everything. You should try asking Him for what you want. I bet He would have much better advice than some low spirit responsible for fungus."

I couldn't help but laugh. Ask God? I could. I could ask God.

Donna's eyes went serious. "There is a supernatural realm, Peggy. It's all around you. But God is in charge of it. If He is all-powerful, all-seeing, all-knowing, then He will be the One Who can guide you and give you answers. He loves His creation. He loves you." She stood up and picked up her purse.

"Bufwhy!" Anna stood in the doorway wiping her sleepy eyes.

Donna beamed. "This is Anna! How pretty she is. How lucky you are to have this beautiful child."

I lifted Anna up onto my hip and Donna placed her hand on Anna's head. "What a blessing she will be to you, in so many ways. What love you will discover because of her. You'll see."

"Thank you for coming over, Donna. This has been a wonderful afternoon."

"I was glad I could catch you. Just remember, if you want something, go to the top!"

"I won't forget."

And just like that, she left. After I set Anna down, I went to the window to see which way she went. But the walkway was empty.

The rest of the afternoon was deliciously calm. I felt so light. As I made dinner, I found myself praying. "God, Donna says I am to talk to you. So here I am." As I looked out my kitchen window, a white seagull drifted by. Anna chattered in the living room while she played with toys. My heart felt flooded with love.

Maybe I would be okay. Maybe I wasn't so alone.

Years later I realized the encounter in my living room may have been an angel in disguise, or at the very least someone God sent to guide me at a very difficult time in my life. At the time, I never thought about asking how she knew where I lived or who gave her my phone number. But because of the visit, I completely forgot about the runes. I must have misplaced them because I never saw them again.

My encounter that afternoon was the beginning of my turning to God in prayer. Over the next several months, my prayers led me into a lifelong relationship with God that grows deeper every day.

Eventually, my marriage to Joey did collapse, and I moved to California with my children where I enjoyed a successful career in the film and television business. I also married a wonderful man who loves and supports me as I continue to pursue my dreams today.

Peggy Patrick Medberry was a literary and talent agent in Hollywood for seventeen years and an associate professor of film and television at Biola University. She currently is a managing partner at Amaris Media International and lives with her family in the Los Angeles area. You can read more of her story in *When God Happens, Volume 1,* and more of her writing at https://seaof glassreflections.com.

ANGEL GLIMPSES

Mrs. Agnes Frazier was the oldest member of Pastor Robert Morgan's church. She was a woman of deep piety and enthusiastic spirituality. At age ninety-five, her health failed, and Pastor Morgan received a call. "Mrs. Agnes is asking for you," said her nurse. When he entered her bedroom, she was almost too weak to look up at him. Her words were indistinct at times, but it soon became clear that she had wanted to see him because she was curious about "these men."

"What men?" the pastor asked.

"I keep seeing these two men," she said.

"What do they look like?"

"Two men, dressed in white from head to foot are standing at the foot of my bed. I don't know what to tell them. What should I say if they ask me something?"

"Tell them," the pastor said at length, "that you belong to Jesus."

That seemed to satisfy her. "Yes," she said, "I'll tell them I belong to Jesus." And shortly afterward, she fell asleep in Christ, and those two angels, he believes, ushered her to Heaven.[10]

CHAPTER SIX

UNLIKELY MESSENGER

BILL MYERS

'd never given angels much thought. Not that I was anti-angel. I mean, I had two friends and a daughter who seemed to have occasional angelic encounters, but angels weren't exactly—how do you say—in my wheelhouse.

My first friend who talked about angels was Ned York, the artistic director of a theater in Los Angeles where I directed my first plays. One time when he was rock climbing, he insisted, he lost both his foot- and handholds. But instead of falling, he felt a hand on his back forcefully shove him against the face of the cliff. The sensation lasted several seconds, long enough for him to find an outcropping to grasp. Once he felt safe, the pressure on his back disappeared, and he was free to continue his climb.

Okay, I figured. *If there really were such things as angels, why not?* Ned hadn't exactly experienced trumpets and wings and flashing swords, but that feeling of a hand on his back seemed good enough for him. And as far as proof? He really didn't have any . . . well, except for the part about still being alive.

Then there was my producer/cameraman, Heinz Fussle. For years, we traveled the world together, from the Amazon to the Andes, to the African Sahara, to—well, you name it, and we've probably filmed there. Nothing creates trust between two men like working side-by-side to accomplish tasks in strange and difficult locations. Well, actually, there is one thing: Having our lives threatened—on more than one occasion. I'll never forget the time in the Philippines when, after we'd hunkered down behind a balcony to hide from what we thought was a band of Muslim terrorists, he told me his angel story.

He was in Switzerland, leaning out a train window to get that perfect shot of the passing Alps. You'd have to know Heinz to understand there are few things he won't do to get that perfect shot. So, he leaned out farther, then a little farther, and suddenly something grabbed him by the shirt collar and yanked him back so hard he slammed into the wall behind him—just as the train passed within inches of a jagged rock wall.

After Heinz checked his camera, then his body (yes, in that order), he turned to thank whoever spared his life. But no one was there. The corridor was completely empty.

Okay, fine. Ned and Heinz were friends who had no reason to lie. I believed them. But both stories were secondhand encounters—something that happened to them, not me.

Things hit closer to home when, a few years later, our four-year-old insisted she saw streaks of light darting about the house. About this same time, I was holding her in church one Sunday when she pointed up front asking, "Daddy, what's the light?"

"What light?" I asked. "Where?"

"There. The one with feathers."

Hmm . . .

Finally, there was the incident with the "glowing fog." She was nine or ten at the time.

I was sitting in the backyard at twilight, out of view of the house, quietly worshiping. Nothing spectacular or uber-holy, just me quietly singing one of those seven-eleven songs—you know, a seven-word chorus repeated eleven times? Anyway, my daughter stepped outside and headed down the walkway until she found me.

"Cool," was all she said.

I looked over and saw her grinning. "'Sup, kiddo?"

She continued approaching. "What's that fog?"

"Fog? What fog?" I glanced around. "There is no fog."

But she barely heard me. "It's all glowy." As she came closer, I could see her staring as if she was watching something. "It's like a cloud thingy. It's all around you."

Whatever she was seeing, I didn't want to frighten her, so I did my best to sound calm and casual. "Well, come over here and join me."

She did, still seeming to stare at something entirely invisible.

"Can you touch it?" I asked.

She stretched out her little hand and gently waved it back and forth. Her eyes moved as if following something washing over her hand, drifting between her fingers. "It's like smoke, but all glowy."

She wasn't living some child's fantasy. Whatever she saw seemed real enough to her. So the investigative reporter in me kicked in.

"Hey, let's try something, okay? A little experiment. I'm going to move to the chair on the other side of this table, okay? And you tell me what happens."

"Okay."

I rose, crossed to the other chair and sat—secretly hoping the glow, or whatever it was, was some sort of aura, the type people occasionally claim to see or artists paint to depict exceptionally great and holy men. (Apparently, *I* was the one living a fantasy.)

"So?" I said. "Am I still glowing?"

Her eyes stayed riveted on the other chair. "It's not you, Daddy."

"Oh." I felt my chances for sainthood slowly ebbing. "Are you sure?"

"Uh-huh." Then, a few seconds later, I saw her eyes slowly drift toward me.

"What's going on?" I asked.

"It's moving. It's surrounding you again."

Well, I thought, *better late than never.*

"How big?" I asked.

She motioned with her hands indicating ten, maybe twelve, feet across. "It's like a little cloud."

A cloud. Now, I'm no Bible scholar, but I remembered reading something about glowing clouds or fog in the Old Testament. Unfortunately, it had nothing to do with a person's "greatness." But I wasn't going to let a little thing like that stop me.

"Okay," I said, "Let's try this." I stood and took several steps to the right. "How about now? Is it moving now?"

She shook her head. "Nope, still there."

I shrugged. Can't fault an egotist for trying.

About this time, Brenda, my wife, called us in for dinner.

"Be right there," I shouted. I turned to my daughter. "Okay," I said. "Let's head back to the house, and you tell me what happens."

She nodded. We started toward the patio, and I kept my eyes on hers. Whatever she watched didn't immediately follow but lagged behind—until she lost its glow in the brightness of the porch lights.

That was it. Nothing else. A couple of years later, she hit puberty, and the lights, feathers, and special effects ceased. Now that she's an adult with her own child, we've discussed her experiences while revisiting the rooms, hallway, and that backyard table. She still insists she saw what she saw, but there has been no encore performance of any kind.

So where did that leave me?

Pretty much where I'd always been—a secondhand observer.

Then came my trip to the Cascade Mountains in Washington State.

As a writer, I'm a research fanatic. Before I start any novel, I will spend weeks, sometimes months, researching the facts and often visiting the locations (particularly if I can use those trips as tax write-offs). I was working on a novel titled *The Presence*—it dealt with a group trapped deep in the forest where, in an experiment, they are incrementally exposed to the presence of God, until—well, it's a long story, and if you feel like contributing to my mortgage, I'm sure it's for sale somewhere online.

Even though I grew up in those very mountains, I wanted to visit and see them with fresh eyes, not as some kid trudging through adolescence but as a writer and—well, I did mention the tax write-off, right? So, I flew up from Los Angeles, rented a car, and traveled deep into the Cascades, far from any town or community. I eventually pulled off near a bridge where I saw two old-timers fishing. We nodded, and I turned to follow an overgrown path along the river. I hiked about three-quarters of a mile upstream until I spotted a fallen cedar stretched over the river— a great place to sit and think. I carefully walked out several yards over the water and eased myself down. Now it was just me, my thoughts—and the mosquitoes.

But instead of noodling on my story or jotting down notes about the surroundings, my mind kept drifting to a bigger issue. These mountains were my roots, where I grew up. And it was here, surrounded by these very peaks, that I was so certain I'd heard God's call on my life.

You see, next to being a famous rock star or an Academy Award winner, I pretty much figured I was going to be a dentist. Don't laugh, it's an admirable profession. Although it may not have remained so had they let me inside people's mouths with drills and sharp, pointy objects. In any case, dental school was the direction I was heading. Until one day, I thought it would be fun to make a promise to always say *yes* to God—regardless what He might ask of me, or how uninformed He might be of the situation. At seventeen, it seemed a harmless promise—particularly because I'd never heard any specific words from Him and never expected to receive any.

Then, I saw the fourth movie of my life. Until then, I'd seen *The Parent Trap* (the original with Haley Mills), *Pollyanna* (Haley Mills, again), and *Pinocchio*. Now, in my freshman year at the University of Washington, I was watching the fourth movie of my life. The title?

The Godfather.

I was beyond shocked. People were shooting and killing each other (Haley Mills would never do that), and blood seemed to gush everywhere. Even more shocking was the ending, when all my friends stood up and cheered as a half-dozen characters were massacred.

I left the theater absolutely numb. Who would have thought one movie could have such an impact on others? Who could believe movies could motivate everyday people to stand up and cheer when characters were being brutally murdered? Someone had to warn God. Wasn't He paying attention? Didn't He see the power? And if the media could be used to create such a negative reaction, imagine what it could do for good. Imagine what would happen if there were movies and television shows inspiring people to love and care for one another. Seriously, God should really get on the ball and call people to make those kinds of things.

The only problem was, every time I told God what He should do, the idea that I should be one of those people to help Him do it bounced back at me. I saw no burning rose bushes, received no angel-grams. But I could not shake that continuous, resonating thought. And, believe me, I tried. We had plenty of arguments. I told God I didn't know how to watch a movie, let alone make one.

But every time I reminded Him how wrong He was and what my chosen profession was to be, He reminded me of His sovereign power and my promise to always say yes.

Long story short: I eventually found myself at a film school in Rome, Italy, studying a subject I knew nothing about in a language I couldn't speak.

That was forty years ago. And now, as I sat alone on that fallen tree over the river, a haunting thought surfaced, one that had been growing stronger and plaguing me more and more. The fact was I'd barely scratched the surface in accomplishing what I thought He'd called me to do. Sure, there were the little films Heinz and I produced, and yes, there was the kids' video series, *McGee and Me*, and a few other projects, but was that it? If so, maybe I'd missed the boat. Maybe I'd devoted my entire life to a mistaken calling. Maybe it was time to rethink my commitment, to forget my lifelong dream and be content to simply write books. Don't get me wrong. There's nothing secondhand about writing books. It's a great life, and I've always loved the folks I worked with. But there is no comparison: a bestselling novel might reach a hundred thousand people (if you're lucky), whereas a single television show might reach thirty million.

Maybe I'd made a mistake. Maybe I'd misheard the Lord. Maybe I was only fooling myself.

Those were the thoughts badgering me when I felt the tree shudder beneath me. I looked over to the river bank and saw an old man with a straggly beard. He wore a clean plaid shirt, hunting vest, and hat, and h

e was standing on my tree.

"Howdy," he said.

"Howdy," I said, pretending not to be startled. It would have been easier had I not noticed the large revolver strapped to his hip.

"Mind if I join you?"

"Sure," I sort of croaked. Did I mention the large revolver?

He continued across the tree and sat down beside me.

We exchanged some pleasantries and small talk which, for the life of me, I can't remember. (I did mention the revolver, right?)

He asked what brought me way out there. I said something about nature and clearing my head. I made a point *not* to mention coming from California because I was well aware of the local sentiment about Californians coming into these parts to spread "their big city ways and liberal morality."

Instead, I pivoted the conversation to him. "What about you?" I asked. "What brings you out here?"

"Well . . ." he coughed and spit. "I'm pretty angry about the media."

I tensed, grateful I had changed subjects before we got to my occupation.

"How—" My voice caught and I cleared it. "The media, you say?"

"Yup."

"How so?"

"Just what it's doing to this great country."

"Really?"

"Yup."

I wish I could remember the details of our conversation (although I remember thinking that was most likely a .44 magnum he was sporting). I do remember he didn't mention any shows by name but spoke more in generalities on how the media chipped away at our values and polluted our culture, especially the kids.

I nodded, thinking of a quote from Jesus I kept above my desk when writing children's projects. ". . . but whoever causes one of these little ones who believe in me to sin, it would be better for him to have a great millstone fastened around his neck and to be drowned in the depth of the sea" (Matt. 18:6 ESV).

We circled the subject a few more minutes while, all the time, I was careful never to become too committal or to let on what I did for a living.

Finally, he concluded, "Folks should really be doin' somethin' 'bout it."

I quietly nodded.

The conversation eventually dropped off, and we sat in silence, taking in the quiet majesty of the place. That's when I noticed a good-sized bear crossing the river thirty to forty yards ahead of us, angling slightly in our direction.

He saw it, too.

"Look at that," I said.

"Yeah." Then, patting his gun, he added, "Good thing I brought this baby along."

I nodded in agreement, although the truth was, I wasn't sure which I feared most—the wild bear in front of us or the odd stranger with the very big gun beside me. We watched as the animal crossed to our side of the river and disappeared into the brush.

After a few more moments of silence, the old-timer finally sighed and struggled to his feet. "Well, I best be getting a move-on."

"Right," I said, grateful our little encounter was ending.

He gave one last nod and walked to the end of the tree, hopped off onto the trail, and headed down the path toward the bridge.

Finally, some peace and quiet. Now, at last, I was alone with just my thoughts.

Well, not exactly alone. There was that bear.

The bear! What was I thinking?

It took less than a minute to gather my stuff. Maybe the old fellow's company wasn't so bad after all. I hightailed it across the tree to join him, throwing more than one look to the bushes into which the bear disappeared.

But the man was nowhere to be found.

"Hello?" I called.

Nothing.

Maybe he was faster than I'd thought. I picked up my pace. "Hello?"

I kept moving, not slowing and not looking back but checking both sides of the path. Still no sign of him.

For reasons that should be clear, my return to the bridge was a lot faster than my departure. But when I arrived, the man was nowhere to be seen. I called out to the fishermen who were still there.

"That older guy," I shouted, "the one with the hat and beard? Where did he go?"

They traded looks and shook their heads.

"You know," I said, "with the hunter's vest? Did he pass you and go farther down river?

"Nobody been on that path 'cept you."

I persisted. "No, I'm talking about this older guy with a beard."

They gave their heads another shake and returned to fishing. I waited a moment in case they felt like changing their minds or their story. They didn't. Finally, I turned and started for my car while checking the mud for any additional tire tracks. There were none.

But the man was too clean to be a hermit in the woods. So how did he get there? How did he leave?

There was no answer, and I wasn't going back into the forest to find one. I opened my car door, climbed inside, and started back down the mountain. What a strange encounter. But to be honest, I hadn't realized the importance of the meeting until I was well down the road, and even then, it didn't fully hit me until several days later.

Here I was, wrestling with the very thing I felt God called me to do, questioning the decades of my service to Him, wondering if I had made some sort of terrible mistake and should give up.

I received an answer. From a man who appeared and then disappeared.

Can I prove the old-timer was an angel? Absolutely not. Particularly if angels need to appear as glow-in-the-dark action figures with wings and feathers.

Then there was the matter of the gun. If he was really an angel, why did he need a gun?

Again, I have no answer—except had that conversation occurred a few thousand years earlier, how would a gun today be any different from a sword back then?

Who knows.

But I know this: When I was discouraged and toyed with the idea of giving up on my life's calling, a strange man appeared from nowhere and set me straight. I gave him no clues about what I was thinking or who I was, but it didn't seem to matter. And once our conversation had served its purpose, he disappeared back into the woods, unseen by anyone else—except maybe a bear.

I am told, in the original Greek language, the translation for the word *angel* is *messenger.* If that's the case, then all I can say is when I was alone, struggling with some serious doubts, a messenger appeared out of the blue and delivered a very strong and much-needed word of encouragement.

Bill Myers is an author/filmmaker whose work has won eighty national and international awards, including the C.S. Lewis Honor Award. His favorite children's book series is *The Incredible World of Wally McDoogle.* And for adults, it's *Eli* (a retelling of the Gospel as if it were today). He can be found hanging out at www. facebook.com/billmyersauthor/.

ANGEL GLIMPSES

The Rev. John G. Paton, a missionary in the New Hebrides Islands, told a story involving the protective care of angels. Hostile natives surrounded his mission headquarters one night, intent on burning out the Patons and killing them. John Paton and his wife prayed all during that terror-filled night that God would deliver them. When daylight came, they were amazed to see the attackers unaccountably leave.

A year later, the chief of the tribe was converted to Christ, and Paton, remembering what happened, asked the chief what kept him and his men from burning down the house and killing them. The chief replied in surprise, "Who were all those men you had there with you?" The missionary answered, "There were no men there; just my wife and me."

The chief argued that they saw many men standing guard, hundreds of big men in shining garments with drawn swords in their hands. They seemed to circle the mission station, so the natives were afraid to attack. Only then did the Rev. Paton realize God had sent His angels to protect them.[11]

CHAPTER SEVEN

ANGEL IN DISGUISE: AUSTIN ACCIDENT

SHIRLANNE GAY-ALEXANDER

I had a really good feeling about the manuscript I just finished. I knew it was going to change my life. I just didn't know how.

The date was Saturday, June 28, 2014. The flyers to promote my new book were finished. And even though we were running behind schedule, I was sure we were going to make it to Austin, Texas, in time for the book convention. I was working with an agent this time around, and she urged me to make sure to get a good buzz going for my book at as many conventions as possible.

My husband, Marvin, and I dropped our kids off at my parents' house and picked up my cousin Shakeer and my two younger brothers, Alan and Brennan, before making the three-hour trip from Houston to Austin. They were coming along to help us pass out flyers.

The weather was rainy when we started our trip, but the sky quickly cleared. We drove to Austin, and even though the convention wasn't what I was expected, we still had a good time. After some brief networking, the five of us left the convention and stopped to have a bite at a local pizzeria before heading over to Sixth Street for a little relaxation.

We hung out and listened to a couple of live bands, then decided to head back to Houston before it got too late. But at about the halfway point, we made a pit stop at a firework stand because the Fourth of July was approaching. I thought the day was going to end perfectly—but I was about to be surprised.

We were about to exit Interstate 10 to fuel up at a gas station when the back tire on our Chevy Tahoe blew out and sent our car careening off the road and onto the grass median. Once the truck reached the other side of the highway, it began to flip. We hadn't run over any nails or glass—the tire we had purchased just two weeks earlier blew out on its own.

My cousin and both brothers were ejected from the vehicle. Thankfully, my husband and I managed to stay inside. Once the flipping stopped, I looked through my shattered window and saw my baby brother Brennan lying on the ground, not moving and possibly not breathing. I forced my door open and ran barefoot through broken glass to his side. Before performing CPR, I scanned the area for my cousin and other brother, Alan. Shakeer was lying on the ground unconscious, but I couldn't see Alan anywhere.

Then, from out of nowhere, Alan came stumbling toward me and my husband, bleeding and unable to breathe. Half of his left ear was gone.

I didn't know what to do. My head was ringing, and hopelessness consumed me. I couldn't save either of my brothers from their dire situations. Then Brennan began to breathe, although his breathing was shallow. But I didn't know how to help Alan.

My husband and I tried to help him breathe by sitting him down and trying to get him to calm down, but we were unsuccessful.

Then he showed up—a black man with a short afro. I didn't notice when he arrived, but there he was. He spoke gently as he laid his hands on our shoulders and calmed me and Marvin. Then he hurried over to Alan and placed a T-shirt against his bleeding ear. He then straightened Alan's body and told him exactly how to breathe. And finally, my brother was able to breathe without struggling.

By that time, people from several cars had pulled over and come to help us. They were able to give the arriving police officers an account of what happened—I could barely speak. As medics strapped me into a stretcher, a police officer came to my side and started asking questions. After he was finished, I asked him to please thank everyone who helped us, especially the man who helped save my brother Alan.

The officer had no idea who I was talking about.

A few minutes later, I asked the emergency medical technician if he saw the black man with the afro, and he shook his head. There was no way that man could have slipped past everyone because he was definitely with us until the first responders arrived. They should have seen him, and the people running to help us should have seen him, too.

But not one other person besides me, Marvin, and Alan saw our mysterious helper.

Alan and I were life-flighted on the same helicopter to the nearest hospital that could take trauma patients, which ironically, was an hour away in downtown Houston. We were nearly home, but not all of us came back that night. Brennan passed away before he reached the hospital. He was only twenty-three years old.

Our sport utility vehicle was crushed like a soda can. My parents and other siblings remember seeing what was left of the Tahoe as they went to identify my brother's body. After seeing the wreckage, they said there was no way any of us should have survived. The trunk had been pushed forward into the backseat. If Brennan, Shakeer, and Alan had not been ejected from the vehicle, all three of them would have been crushed.

My little brother was only in that SUV to help me with my dream of becoming a writer. But as painful as losing a brother is, that disaster could have been worse if the stranger with the afro hadn't helped Alan. I might have lost two brothers that day. Alan suffered a fractured spine and a ruptured lung, and the stranger's action might have saved his life.

A kind lady held my hand and prayed with me as I lay strapped onto that stretcher, but she couldn't recall the man with the afro when I asked if she got him to pray with us, too. But whether he was an unselfish man (with, apparently, the power to appear and disappear) or an angel sent from God, I will always be grateful for the assistance he gave my family that day.

Shirlanne Gay Alexander was born in Houston on June 16, 1983, to parents Anet and Conrad Gay. She is the oldest girl of seven siblings, with one sister and five brothers. Her Trinidadian parents encourage all their children to love the Almighty and his Son, follow their dreams, and always keep an open mind. In 2012, she married Marvin Alexander. Together they live in Houston with their two wonderful children, Kaylann and Marvin Jr., and their two dogs, Marley and Smokey.

ANGEL GLIMPSES

It should be (but it is not) unnecessary to add that a belief in angels, whether good or evil, does not mean a belief in either as they are represented in art and literature. Devils are depicted with bats' wings and good angels with birds' wings, not because anyone holds that moral deterioration would be likely to turn feathers into membrane, but because most men like birds better than bats.

—C. S. Lewis[12]

CHAPTER EIGHT

MORE THAN A T-SHIRT

CHRISTOPHER MOYA

The summer of 1982 held a great many delights, as summers tend to do for seven-year-olds, and mine was no different but for one remarkable exception that began with a sea-worthy inner tube at a creek head in Zion National Park. To hear my gregarious mother tell the story, with idiosyncratic gusto, is a bit like listening to a sorceress recount a legend. And although she may remember certain aspects in greater detail, the whole experience would seem mythical indeed if not for the most crucial parts imprinted on my own memory as vividly as today's lunch.

Having made our way north after a brief stay in Las Vegas, Nevada, Interstate 15 delivered my family across the Utah border. My detached but full-of-dry-wit dad handled the wheel of our blue Ford Zephyr station wagon, ever mindful of the tent trailer coupled just behind us. Somewhere between the zenith of a July afternoon and twilight's fading embers, we pulled into Zion's

South Campground and readied the trailer, with plenty of good-natured grumbling between my parents as my dad continually wiped his forehead with the wrist of his glove. Finally, the thing sat anchored among the trees in expanded glory, ready to receive us for the night.

Much of my memory of the trip is framed by the shady arbors and green underbrush punctuating the campsite. My mind also fills with other minor images, such as the metal feet of the trailer planted obliquely like legs of a lunar lander, or the mustard yellow of the box toilet, which required a daily jettison to make the living space livable. But none of those memories comes close to the vivid impression of the lazy afternoon when we threw on swim trunks and bathing suits, grabbed our oversized beach towels, and ambled down the side of a nearby ravine with one of the camp's rented inflatables—a black inner tube that might as well have been a schooner, being nearly as tall as me when upright.

The Virgin River, which wound through the canyon, was dreadfully cold. If memory serves, my older brother Anthony threatened several times, as older brothers do, to toss me in without the gradual submersion most people prefer. I protested, as younger brothers do, and Anthony went first, which may have been his plan all along, not that an older brother needs a reason to do anything first.

With my mother standing in three feet of water, he rode the inner tube down the 100-yard stretch that must have been the length of the campground. And as planned, Mom caught him and sent him back up the bank with inner tube in hand. It was my turn next. I waded cautiously into the water, bracing myself against the cold, as the water gleamed with that disorienting sense of motion. If I remember correctly, Anthony helped me into position and released me, the slap of cold water on my lower half matched a moment later by the exhilaration of the tube's speed. Honestly, anything more than the static bobbing that takes place in your average pool is enough to make a juvenile heart soar. Again, Mom was waiting and grabbed me before the inner tube could zip past her.

The turn-taking continued a couple times until Anthony expressed his wish to catch me. Mom agreed, and my brother was allowed to stand guard and make sure I didn't drift past the mark—an important mark, too, since we already heard the caveat from a park attendant not to drift beyond the camp because the water would get choppy, and a perilous drop-off awaited those who went too far.

So, with Anthony fully committed and waist deep, waiting to catch me, the whole endeavor seemed airtight. Yet something must have drawn his attention because, after another exhilarating run, I passed the retrieval point with Anthony nowhere in sight.

I recall not thinking the situation too serious at first and wondered if Mom or Dad might be waiting farther downstream to pull me out. But a chilling fear awoke in me as all trace of the camp disappeared, and I rode the inner tube into a region that appeared to be utter wilderness.

Over the next five minutes, the babbling stream turned swift and foamy. Though only waist-deep in most spots, the current became so fast that getting out of the tube seemed more precarious than staying put. Mom appeared, and I can still hear the distant sound of her voice as she raced along the canyon's edge. Remembering the drop-off, my seven-year-old self began to pray, perhaps more intensely than ever before, asking the Good Lord, in His grace, to deliver me from a fall that would hurt me at best and kill me at worst. I closed my eyes and prayed, convinced of the danger but not yet overtaken by the certainty of death.

The inner tube spun and pitched furiously, I feared being upended and dumped into the churning water. My heart pounded as fear turned to panic, and my eyes shifted from one side of the ravine to the other, looking for something to take hold of but finding nothing. Occasionally I saw a rock too slippery to grab, but that was all. I was surrounded by endless swirling waters as the river raced like a juggernaut down the canyon.

Not until a gently protruding rock suddenly hooked the tube did a ray of hope shoot through my mind. I sat there, breathing hard and groping the algae-coated stone, the water lapping ferociously over my arms and slapping me in the face so I could hardly see what was happening. I took stock and realized that without other rocks to hold while I made my way to land, I would be at the mercy of the river.

I resolved to take the only course of action left.

I pushed the inner tube off the rock and was swept away once again. As the tube could not decide which way to toss me, I struggled to face downstream. At this point, for the first time I realized I might make the evening news, a swift and sorry accident. I would be a cautionary tale to other seven-year-olds who tubed in the Virgin River, a frequently cited reminder to take care not to fall victim to one of nature's meaner forces.

With this thought wreaking havoc in my mind and resigning myself to the fact the turbulent water was totally unnavigable, I gave myself to prayer, closing my eyes and asking God, in simple but earnest words, to save my life. I asked Him to do what I had, to that point, only heard about in stories—something beyond the natural, to *make a way*. I asked for a miracle.

I can't remember how long I prayed or how long my eyes were closed. What I do recall with utter clarity is that the inner tube entered a quiet stretch of water at a shady break in the tree line above the canyon. No sooner had I noticed this than I felt a compelling force push my inner tube. Against the flow of the water, something suddenly and conspicuously pulled my tube to the right. This new trajectory carried me to the edge of a long sandbar, one protected by a dense coat of branches and leaves.

I crept gratefully out of the inner tube, never so glad in all my short life for the feel of loamy earth, for sticks and mud and all the raw, elemental substances that meant I was safe. I crawled toward the riverbank and climbed a formidable wall of interlocking branches. Because it was my only way out of the ravine, I grabbed hold of the vines and slowly ascended, twigs and rocky protrusions scraping my arms and legs as I went.

Finally, I reached the top, where my mother was waiting to take my hand. And only now am I realizing the inner tube was decidedly *not* pushed to the left, where my mother would have had no way to reach me. (Later, I learned she navigated several backyards and fenced-in properties to get to me.)

My energy spent, Mom pulled me out of the ravine and into a giant hug, covering me with grateful congratulations laced with loving care, as only a mother can.

I spent the rest of the afternoon bundled in one of the trailer bunks. Despite being dreadfully shaken, I'll never forget my sense of relief or the notion of having been graciously and supernaturally delivered. I said as much to my mother, who gave praise to God for the same. I knew I'd received the miracle I prayed for, but that wasn't a life-changing experience at the time. I still went on to ask all the big questions as a teenager and to wrestle with questions of faith.

What I later came to understand about my experience in the Virgin River was it counted as evidence. It happened. And because it happened, it mattered. It had to be counted in the revolution of my worldview that occurred some years later, standing in contrast to naturalism, the academic name for the assumption all phenomena are preceded by a physical cause. The leap I finally made as a young adult was to embrace the idea that reality may be larger than what is observable, and my experience in the inner tube gave me grounds to believe in a force that interferes with the chain of physical causes and effects. Call it supernaturalism, and the interference a miracle.

My experience convinced me in the same way Jesus's miracles convinced the first-century disciples. Although some may react with rigid skepticism and call my testimony no more credible than someone whose UFO sighting turns out to be nothing more than a wisp of light from a radio tower. Testimony is all I have, after all. And the fact that I'm still here. Had I not been saved by a miracle, I wouldn't be.

So, with what lesson did I walk away? Wilderness excursions are notorious for their souvenir T-shirts, which are often imprinted with "I Survived the Snake" or "I climbed _____ Mountain, and all I got was this lousy shirt." My takeaway was more than a thrill and far more than a hat or a T-shirt. My worldview might not have taken shape the moment I got out of the water, but the experience was seminal, precipitating droves of intellectual push-ups eventually leading to an awareness of the Creator. As gratifying as it was to be pushed toward the shore and never reach the drop-off, I realized the maelstrom of chance is insufficient to be the initiator of meaning, life, and the universe. I came to understand a benevolent intelligence doesn't merely intercede in reality, but is uniquely responsible for designing and sustaining it. This epiphany was a game-changer, a marvelous first step in answering the question *Why am I alive in the first place?*

Could the Bible with which I was raised be true? A history, as opposed to an anthology of fables? Is Christ the lone victor in conquering the brokenness we each inherit. Whose victory brings us back into relationship with the Father, into His family, as it were? What did I walk away with if not the seed of *yes*, the germ that would grow for years and chase me down until my rational mind was convinced of a truth it could no longer deny? Some of us walk away from perilous moments with gnarly scars or checks on a bucket list. But what of the souvenir that transforms understanding?

My gain was an awareness of the truth and the conviction to walk in that until the hour I finally face that frontier of the spirit and join in the inheritance of Christ. When that day comes, I imagine I will find I merely sojourned a while between that seaworthy inner tube and eternity. What God gives me to do in the middle is to bend like a reed in the wind, because no force of nature or human intent can withstand His purpose.

In this vapor called life, we're liable to believe not only that nothing has purpose but also our own perception is what curates truth instead of what God has revealed. My answer? The reply sown at seven, though it took years to shape me—

Not a chance.

Chris Moya grew up the youngest of two boys in the Southern California 'burbs. Although he's taught high school mathematics for the past sixteen years, he has always been drawn to the beauty of the written word. He resides in Westlake Village with his wife Laura and their toddling son Elliot, whose exuberance and curiosity make him both a handful and an endless joy.

ANGEL GLIMPSES

When Robert Morgan Met Corrie Ten Boom

Years ago, I popped into a hotel elevator and found myself standing beside the famous Christian writer and Nazi death camp survivor, Corrie Ten Boom. I recognized her at once, having read her books and seen her on television. When I introduced myself, instead of giving me a usual greeting, she squinted at me as only an old woman can squint and asked with a Dutch accent: "Young man, have you ever seen an angel?"

"No," I replied, startled. "Not that I know of."

"Well, I have," she declared. And in the time our elevator took to reach the bottom floor, she told me of a time when she was smuggling Bibles into Communist Eastern Europe. The border guard was checking everyone's luggage, and she knew her load of Bibles would surely be discovered. In alarm, she prayed, "Lord, You have said that You would watch over Your Word. Now, please watch over Your Word that I am smuggling."

Suddenly, as she looked at her suitcase, it seemed to glow with light. No one else saw it, but to her it was unmistakable. There was an aura of light wrapped around that suitcase.

Her turn came at customs, and the guard, who had so vigilantly opened and inspected every piece of everyone else's luggage, glanced at her bags, shrugged, and waved her through.

It was an angel, she told me, who had helped her deliver God's Word behind the Iron Curtain.[13]

CHAPTER NINE

DON'T JUDGE AN ANGEL BY ITS TATTOOS

APRIL CHAPMAN

A friend called and asked if I would come help pray over her house. Not only had weird things been happening in her home, but she felt as if she couldn't pray there. I was invited to join the team of prayer warriors because my daughters and I had recently moved out of a home that put me through a crash course in the spiritual realm and how to pray powerfully and effectively.

Unfortunately, after I returned from the prayer session at her house, the peace we enjoyed disappeared. Something flung crosses off the walls, pictures mysteriously fell, and more—the kind of stuff you'd see in a movie. I obviously had ticked off someone or something enough to follow me home.

Two weeks later, the spiritual attack was still underway at our house. My daughters and I were constantly arguing, and the usual go-with-the-flow atmosphere in our home seemed . . . infiltrated. I called my best friend to ask her to pray for my family because we were under spiritual assault. I told her about the strange events and the constant bickering. I didn't tell her about *my* internal conflict. I was being bombarded with negative thoughts. Because I am a perpetual "Pollyanna," pessimism is not my normal attitude. That very morning, however, for the first time I silently agreed with the inner dialogue that had been bombarding me for weeks:

> *You don't need to publish your book.*
> *Who are you to be a speaker?*
> *It's just pride. God doesn't need you.*
> *If you were really a good, humble Christian, you wouldn't want to do any of those things.*

My friend and I prayed about the external attacks, and then I headed to my office. I didn't know it, but God was already in the process of answering our prayer.

The night before I received a text notification from a man asking if I still had my planter for sale. Planter? I didn't remember putting a planter up for sale, but apparently, I had. I texted, "Sure," and agreed to meet him in a parking lot the next day.

The man arrived in a beat-up old truck. He had a long white beard and arms covered in tattoos of the skull-and-crossbones variety. He was the kind of guy you expect to be riding a Harley, decked out in leather from head to toe. All I could think was *I'm going to make this exchange as quickly as possible and get back to my nice, safe office.* Then, as I walked toward him to make the exchange, I heard Christian music playing in his truck.

Lesson learned: Don't judge a book by its cover—or its tattoos.

After making a comment about liking his music, I headed back toward my office. I was at least fifteen feet away when I heard, "Hey April—I want to tell you what I'm gonna do with this planter."

Wait—how did that guy know my name?

I slowly turned as he began telling me how he felt compelled to create a serenity garden, a place to pray and experience God's peace.

At that moment, as this strange giant of a man talked about a serenity garden, I felt God speak to my spirit: *This is a divine encounter, are you going to accept it?*

My heart instantly changed gears. I moved from trying to understand why this man wouldn't let me walk away to feeling excitement about whatever God planned.

The conversation went from shallow to deep in moments, and he was doing 80 percent of the talking. That alone was a miracle—I'm usually doing 80 percent of the talking! Soon, we were discussing the spiritual realm, and he was teaching and speaking truth that resonated with everything God was teaching me over the past year.

When I told this stranger my family had been under attack for the last two weeks, his answer sent chills down my spine. He looked me directly in the eyes and said, "Yes. That is what is happening."

Not "Yeah—that could be happening." Not "Well-—that would make sense."

Nope. He was 100 percent certain. And in the core of my being, I knew he was right.

The man proceeded to tell me everything in my past had not happened by accident, and God was going to use all of it. This, coming from a man who didn't know my life was like a *Lifetime* movie. Hours before, I had agreed to walk away from God's call to write and speak about my experiences. God wasn't going to let me even get through the day without dealing with my denial of my true calling.

Twenty minutes into the conversation, I felt the Holy Spirit speak to me again: *I want you to ask him to pray over you.* Now, I have no problem praying over someone I've just met, but many

Christians are uncomfortable praying in front of others, so I make it a practice never to ask others to pray aloud. However, since the Holy Spirit was asking . . .

I took a deep breath. "Would you be willing to pray for me?"

His face lit up. "Absolutely." He got out of his truck and took hold of my hands. He began to pray, I could feel the presence of the Holy Spirit around us. His strong voice was full of authority yet soft and comforting at the same time. Then he placed his hand on my head and said, "God *has* called you. He *has* anointed you. And it is time to go now."

After he finished praying, he brought me into a big bear hug and told me to pray over my kids when I got home. Later, I did, and all the spiritual harassment ended immediately. Peace returned to our home.

As I walked away, I kept thinking about how he used my name over and over again. *April, April, April*—as if he knew me, yet I had no idea what *his* name was. I was reminded of how Jesus knows our name, and speaks it intimately, before we ever know His. Then I realized I'd just met an angel.

As soon as I reached my office, I pulled out my phone to see his profile on the app through which he had contacted me. There it was, right at the top: Gabriel.

Only two angels are named in the Bible: Michael, the archangel who leads angel armies into battle, and Gabriel, whose name means *Messenger from God*.

Not long after our meeting, Gabriel sent me this text through the app:

Deuteronomy 31:6— Be strong and of good courage, do not fear nor be afraid of them; for the LORD your God, He is the One who goes with you. He will not leave you nor forsake you! God's blessings over you and your family always.

—Gabriel

I responded: "Thank you so much for living up to your name today—Messenger of God—and saying exactly what my heart needed to hear."

His last message to me?

Psalm 91:11.

Good night, April.

I looked up the verse as soon as I could. Psalm 91:11—"For he will order his angels to protect you wherever you go."

April Chapman is a Christian author and retreat speaker who encourages women to kick fear to the curb and walk in faith. She cherishes spending time with her three teenage daughters, who manage to keep her feeling young and old simultaneously. You can find more information about April and her ministry at www.april-chapman.com.

ANGEL GLIMPSES

In her book, *Evidence Not Seen: A Woman's Miraculous Faith in the Jungles of World War II*, Darlene Deibler Rose tells of her experiences after the Japanese invasion of the island of New Guinea during World War II.

When the Japanese invaded the island, her husband was dragged away—she never saw him again—and she was left with another woman in a rat-infested house on the outskirts of the jungle. Japanese troops were everywhere and so were ruthless bandits.

One night, her rest was disturbed by what she thought were rats. She heard them moving around in the living room, in the dining room, and along the halls. She tried to ignore them, but when she heard a book fall to the floor, that did it. "Margaret," she called to her fellow worker, "grab your dressing gown. We'll light the lamps and have another go at the rats. I've been hearing them from one end of the house to the other."

A hall ran the full length of the house. When she pulled open the bedroom door, in the dim light of a little night lamp, she saw someone swish past her. Stepping into the hall for a better look, she found herself face-to-face with a Boegis bandit.

He was wearing a black sarong that he flung over his shoulder to free his machete. With one fluid movement, the knife was extracted from his belt and held up in a striking position.

On impulse, Darlene rushed at him, and the man inexplicably turned and ran down the hall, through the bathroom, across the porch, and into the trees with Darlene hot on his heels. Other bandits appeared, and together they fled. Darlene stopped dead in her tracks and whispered, "Lord, what a stupid thing for me to do!"

Instantly a verse flashed into her mind: "The angel of the Lord encamps round about them that fear him and delivers them."

From that night on, Darlene slept with a club at the foot of her bed, but she never had to use it. The bandits returned several nights later but never entered the house. She was not disturbed again. She suspected the gardener among the bandits, and after the war, she asked him about it. Yes, he had been one of the culprits.

Darlene later wrote, "When I asked him why they had never entered the house again, he answered incredulously, 'Because of those people you had there—those people in white who stood about the house.'

"The Lord had put His angels around us. He had delivered."[14]

CHAPTER TEN

THE ROAD LESS TRAVELED

SANDRA BYRD

O ur family was in London for a holiday—work and pleasure—and we rented a tiny flat with a lovely view of the Thames but in an area my daughter declared to be teetering on "the edge of sketch." After a day's sightseeing, we deposited our teenagers at that flat while my husband and I set out for a stroll. There was a hole-in-the-wall restaurant not too far away, I explained, that I read had wonderful takeaway food. We could bring some back for dinner.

We set out walking, and walking, and walking, and it wasn't too long until we realized we were blindingly lost. We had a small map that didn't help much once we were in the thinner arteries of the city, in a less traveled neighborhood that clearly recognized us as not of their own. There were few people walking, fewer still loitering in door stops, smoking as they warily eyed us.

We stood in an empty intersection, turning this way and that, wondering what to do next and praying for help. After a nearly complete clockwise spin, my husband turned back from looking down an empty street and was surprised to find a small, elderly man with a neat white beard appear from nowhere; he stood on the broad stoop of a locked and barred door, an area I had just glanced at and found to be vacant.

Approaching my husband, he asked in a thick Scots accent, "Which way are ye going?"

"That way," my husband said hesitantly, pointing west.

"That's where I'm going too," the stranger replied.

"No," I corrected as I turned back around, certain the restaurant was in another direction. "That way." I pointed southeast.

"That's where I'm going, too," the Scotsman said.

My husband and I exchanged a glance above the stranger's head. Didn't he know where he was going, either? He could certainly not have been going both west and southeast. The guile with which he answered both questions, in contrast, made me uneasy.

I explained we were Americans—he grinned; clearly, he could already guess this by our accents. We wanted to locate a restaurant I read about online but was a challenge to find.

"Follow me," he commanded. "I know the place." I was nervous, but what choice did we have? Others gathered nearby, eyeing us warily, perhaps hungrily.

I looked the Scotsman over and noticed my husband did, too. The man was slight, perfectly dressed in an expensive navy wool coat with a tartan scarf wrapped around his neck and a blue felt hat on his head. Because he was slight, my husband could definitely "take him" if need be, should we get into trouble following him. I glanced at the man's shoes. They were well worn, almost falling apart, a distinct contrast to his well-cared-for clothing. I wrote it off to Scots frugality, and we followed him.

Within a minute or two, he led us down an alley that appeared completely deserted. *Was he leading us somewhere to be jumped?* The alley was off the beaten path, and the buildings were so high on either side we would be completely hidden from view.

I glanced at my husband, who walked in the middle, making light, awkward conversation with the man and me. My husband nodded that we should continue. I was certain he, like me, remembered the others in the street we'd just left, with not-so-friendly faces.

After a few minutes of twists and turns down an alley that looked both Dickensian in its grit and modern in its gated doorways, we arrived at an opening to a long street, nearly abandoned, with business after business on either side shuttered and barred off, a long, nearly unbroken row with no further openings until the street met with a busy crossroad about a half mile down.

We stood in front of the restaurant, and the man nodded. "Here you are, then." He looked down the long street. "When you've finished, you walk straight and quickly till you come to the main road, and then turn right." He had not asked to where we were returning, so I did not know how he knew which way we should go. I then realized we hadn't even mentioned the name of this restaurant, but it was, indeed, the one we sought!

He spoke up again. "Do not go back the way you came," he said in a voice much stronger than could be expected from a slight, elderly man. "It's *nae* safe for you."

We nodded, still somewhat bewildered and stunned, and said nothing further but stepped inside the restaurant.

Within a second, I said to my husband, "Oh! We forgot to thank him!" I turned and went outside, but the man was gone. I quickly walked several steps in one direction, and then the next, but there were no breaks in the walls of businesses, and none of the surrounding buildings was even open; our Scotsman was nowhere to be found. Within the previous few seconds, he had disappeared.

My heart quickened, and I felt wrapped in a holy hush; within my spirit, I knew. He'd been sent to help us, presented in a way that would make us feel safe and comforted, but in the well-worn shoes of someone who walked many miles in service.

We bought our delicious food and walked quickly toward the road, as we'd been instructed. It was true, then, what Scripture promised: Angels are sent to guard our way (Ps. 91:11; Exod. 23:20), to protect and guide us, to serve, protect, and be messengers of God: "Do not go back the way you came, it's *nae* safe for you," is timeless truth for all who walk the path of faith, is it not?

Angels are not just for "back then" and not just for others, but for us, all of us, here and now, those of us who will inherit salvation (Heb. 1:14).

Billy Graham, in his book *Angels: God's Secret Agents*, recalled a similar situation wherein a group of American troops trapped up north during the Korean war were freezing, starving, and lost. After prayer and praise, they found themselves suddenly confronted with an English-speaking South Korean who led them through the mountains to safety behind their own lines. "When they looked up to thank him," Graham writes, "they found that he had disappeared."

I read this account some years after our London encounter, but it resonated perfectly with our experience.

Life can be difficult; we can become lost, bewildered, confused, and in dangers of various sorts. God, however, promises he will never leave us; He is a very present help in times of trouble (Ps. 46:1). Sometimes, to our unexpected pleasure, that help arrives in angelic form, of which we mostly, at the time, remain unaware (Heb. 13:2).[15]

Award-winning and bestselling author **Sandra Byrd** has published fifty books in the fiction and nonfiction markets. For nearly two decades, Sandra has shared her secrets with the many writers she edits, mentors, and coaches. She and her husband live in Seattle near their grown children and with their Havanese circus dog; please visit Sandra at www.sandrabyrd.com.

ANGEL GLIMPSES

Charles Herbert Lightoller was tall, sun-bronzed, and handsome, possessing a deep, pleasant speaking voice. His mother died during his infancy, his father abandoned him, and he ran off to sea at the age of thirteen. By 1912, he was a respected seaman for the White Star Line and was assigned to the maiden voyage of the greatest ocean liner ever built, the *Titanic.*

He was just drifting off to sleep on April 14 when he felt a bump in the ship's forward motion. Hopping from his bunk, he soon learned the *Titanic* had struck an iceberg. As the horrors of that night unfolded, Lightoller finally found himself standing on the roof of the officer's quarters, the water lapping at his feet, as he helped any and all around him into lifeboats. Finally, there was nothing left for Lightoller to do but jump from the roof into the freezing waters of the North Atlantic.

The shock of the twenty-eight-degree water against his sweating body stunned him. As he struggled to regain his bearing and swim away from the ship, he was suddenly sucked back and pinned against a ventilation grate at the base of a funnel that went all the way down to Boiler Room Six. He was stuck, drowning, and going down with the ship.

Suddenly, Psalm 91:11 came clearly to his mind: *For He shall give His angels charge over you, to keep you in all your ways . . .*

At that moment, a blast of hot air exploded from the belly of the ship, shooting Lightoller like a missile to the surface of the ocean. At length, he managed to grab a piece of rope attached to the side of an overturned lifeboat and float along with it until he pulled himself on top of the upside-down boat.

He turned and watched the last moments of the *Titanic.* Her stern swung up in the air until the ship was in "an absolutely perpendicular position." Then she slowly sank into the water, with only a small gulp as her stern disappeared beneath the waves.

There were about thirty men atop the lifeboat, and together they recited the Lord's Prayer. Then Lightoller took command of the boat and guided them to safety.[16,17]

CHAPTER ELEVEN

WHEN ANGELS RIDE ALONG

TIM RITER

Mark, my college roommate, looked up as we lounged around the house we rented for our senior year at Pepperdine. "I wonder what Ron's up to in the northern country?"

Without thinking, I responded, "No idea. Why don't we head up there after graduation and find out?" Graduation would arrive in less than a month.

Mark called my bluff, we kicked the idea around for a week or two, and the game was on until Mark realized he couldn't afford it. I thought I might be able to swing the trip alone, but while driving up the Harbor Freeway in downtown Los Angeles, my trusty car abruptly became untrusty. A lady in the adjoining lane braked, and her faulty brakes propelled her into my Falcon. She had no insurance. Trip off.

But during finals week, a friend called. "Some of us need a break from the books and *Easy Rider* is playing in Inglewood. You guys wanna come along?"

I had little interest in motorcycles, but I'd ridden a Honda Trail 90 the summer before and liked it, plus the iconic biker cult film featuring sex and drugs sounded better than books. We watched Peter Fonda and Dennis Hopper ride their choppers from Southern California (SoCal) to New Orleans, Louisiana, good times and tough times intertwined, to a very bad end.

The movie entranced me. Not the sex and drugs, but the freedom of traveling on two wheels.

An idea burst upon me like inspiration: I'd work for a month or so, save enough to buy a bike, and head to Canada for a month before grad school started. I talked to a friend who rode, got some tips on safety, riding, and maintenance. Three weeks after buying a Honda 350 Scrambler, I took off—way too early. I knew almost nothing about riding or bikes. Not enough to know the dangers.

Heading up California's famed Highway 1 captivated me: the grandeur of the redwoods hugging the road and blocking the sun. The red clay sticking to the tires after a summer rain in Weaverville. The gentle aroma of onions in a truck half a mile ahead aroused my hunger.

I camped on a deserted Oregon beach, with sand dunes for cover and the Pistol River for bathing and drinking water. Lying in my sleeping bag on the Olympic Peninsula, pulling blackberries off the vines within arm's reach—heaven. Meeting locals on the Avenue of the Giants and accepting their offer of a bed and a hot shower. A bowl of hot chili pushing back the chill of riding on a foggy day.

I fell in love with riding. I loved being embedded in nature. I was so entranced I focused on glories more than my responsibilities. My infatuation with the experience hid the dangers of biking. Not even finding a flat tire on my bike after touring a castle in Victoria, British Columbia, overcame my love for the road.

I gloried in the flat forests on the road to Banff and enjoyed the responsiveness of the bike. I loved how it took the curves like body-surfing a wave back in SoCal. The bike rode well, even though it was loaded with a backpack strapped to the sissy bar, and often I'd do a dozen linked S-turns on straight stretches of road, exulting in the sensory overload of road and bike and gravity and centrifugal force and acceleration.

Until.

Heading south out of Banff toward Idaho in the magnificent Canadian Rockies, just above Radium Hot Springs, life caught up with me. Taking full advantage of the capabilities of the bike, I headed into a long, sweeping right turn. I barely noticed the thirty-five-mph sign while doing sixty mph. Okay, maybe more. But I'd done it before. I told myself those speed signs were for cars, not nimble bikes.

I grinned as I flowed through the turn, then the bike shook and jerked up and to the left. The rear tire skidded across the pavement, and in a flash, I remembered some basic high school physics lesson and realized what happened and the likely outcome. My heart sank.

Like nearly all bikes back then, the chain drive of my Honda 350 Scrambler needed daily maintenance—lubing and tightening the chain as it stretched. Well, I'd fallen more in love with the union of biker, bike, and road than with maintenance. The chain didn't like being ignored. Having stretched too much, it slipped off the sprocket, jammed, and locked the rear wheel. Mix together a high center of gravity, a tight curve, immediate and complete braking, and an inexperienced rider, and you get a recipe for going down. Hard.

Not knowing what to do, I somehow kept the bike upright, leaned right without it sliding out from under me, and corrected with a slight lean to the left and then to the right, until the Scrambler skidded to a stop at the side of the road—upright all the time, and all under ten seconds. Maybe five. Adrenaline-induced trembling immobilized me when I realized I should have gone down with significant injuries—or worse.

After calming down enough to move, I loosened the rear wheel to lessen the tension, disconnected the chain at the master link, and untangled it from the rear sprocket. Then I reconnected the chain and put it back on the sprocket. I adjusted the tension of the chain by moving the rear wheel to the back

After that incident, I never let a day go by without maintaining that chain.

But I think I might have just stretched the truth. I'm not sure I did keep that bike upright. By the laws of physics, I should have fallen. A high center of gravity ensured it. A rookie rider almost guaranteed it.

God never spoke to me about this in a special message or revelation, but I'm convinced an angel, or several, kept me on the bike that day. Humility may not be one of my greater gifts, but my then-minimal skills couldn't have kept the bike from sliding on asphalt. I hadn't ridden long enough. I never even came close to going down, so I didn't have a clue about what to do.

God didn't owe me anything that day because I'd left God behind a couple of years before. I was raised in church, but the questions that arrived with my college years wiped out my shallow faith and sent me on a search for truth. On a chilly day in February, six months after my adventure near Radium Hot Springs, I knelt beside my twin bed in grad school and told God He could do whatever he desired in my life. I wondered if the angels were riding along so I'd be around the next February.

That experience changed my life. Physically, I learned to not let gear and equipment and maintenance slide, or I'd be apt to slide on pavement. Spiritually, I learned I live in a spiritual world in which God plays an active part. Maybe He doesn't always act as dramatically as He did near Radium Hot Springs on that August day, but that's okay. Sometimes I prefer the low-key approach.

One of these days, when I meet God face to face, I'm going to ask Him how many angels were riding along with me that day.

Temecula, in SoCal, serves as **Tim Riter's** base, where he lives with his wife Sheila and cat Allie. Yeah, intentional, but it's a long story. He served as a pastor for several decades, then as a college professor, and his tenth book came out in 2019, *God, a Motorcycle, and the Open Road*, a story-driven devotion that shows how God appears in daily events. You can catch his weekly posts on Unconventional, at timriter.com.

ANGEL GLIMPSES

Dobie Gadient, a schoolteacher for thirteen years, decided to travel across America and see the sights she taught about. Traveling alone in a truck with camper in tow, she launched out. One afternoon, while she was rounding a curve on Interstate 5 near Sacramento, California, in rush-hour traffic, a water pump blew on her truck. She was tired, exasperated, scared, and alone. In spite of the traffic jam she caused, no one seemed interested in helping.

Leaning up against the trailer, she prayed, "Please, God, send me an angel, preferably one with mechanical experience." Within four minutes, a huge Harley drove up, ridden by an enormous man sporting long, black hair, a beard, and tattooed arms. With an incredible air of confidence, he jumped off and went to work on the truck, without even glancing at Dobie. Within another few minutes, he flagged down a larger truck, attached a tow chain to the frame of the disabled Chevy, and whisked the whole 56-foot rig off the freeway onto a side street, where he calmly continued to work on the water pump.

The intimidated schoolteacher was too dumbfounded to talk, especially when she read the paralyzing words on the back of his leather jacket: "Hell's Angels—California." As he finished his task, she finally got up enough courage to say, "Thanks so much," and carry on a brief conversation. Noting her surprise at the whole ordeal, he looked her straight in the eye and advised, "Don't judge a book by its cover. You may not know who you're talking to." With that, he smiled, closed the hood of the truck, and straddled his Harley. With a wave, he was gone as fast as he had appeared.[18]

CHAPTER TWELVE

ANGELS WE HAVE HEARD ON HIGH

MELODY CARLSON

M y grandmother was not a religious woman. Oh, she was good and kind and generous and loving—the sort of woman who regularly visited neighborhood shut-ins. She was the best quintessential grandma imaginable. She knew how to make saltwater taffy, crispy clam fritters, and Mulligan stew. She knew how to hunt, fish, garden, and sew almost anything. She even knew how to repair small appliances. She was clever and witty and fun. She was like a second mother to me. I can honestly say I wouldn't be who I am today without the influence of Grandma.

Because my parents divorced when I was young, leaving my mother to be a single working woman, my sister and I spent most of our spare time at Grandma's house. That added up to many summers, long weekends, and memorable holidays in the coastal

Victorian house. And we were always glad to go there. It was a magical place where Grandma always made us feel welcomed, loved, and completely at home.

Grandma was never a churchgoer. For that matter, no one in my extended family seemed particularly interested in church. Growing up without any religious influences, I declared myself an atheist at the enlightened age of twelve. How could God exist in a world that was so messed up? Who needed Him anyway?

Apparently, I did. Because after several years of a "godless" mixed-up life, I realized it was not working for me. In a world ripe with seventies-style immoralities, I was feeling progressively lost. So, after some sincere searching—and a spiritual awakening—I became a Christian in high school. It was truly a darkness-to-light conversion and so life-changing that I wanted everyone around me to experience the same wonderful thing, including my grandmother.

So, as a well-meaning but fairly naïve new believer, I became concerned for Grandma's "spiritual condition." As a result, I subjected her to a bit of immature and ill-informed evangelism. And my dear grandma simply took it in stride. I'm sure she even chuckled with amusement when I wasn't looking.

Years passed, and my grandma continued being a good, kind, generous, and loving person, and for a few years, she even attended Sunday school with a group of sweet elderly ladies. She kept her Bible handy, too. But, for some reason—probably because I was still a well-meaning but somewhat naïve Christian—I continued to feel a slight concern for her spiritual condition. Looking back now, I just have to shake my head at my ignorance and arrogance. But as I gave Grandma spiritual books to read and the occasional "sermon," I know I meant well.

As Grandma grew older, passing through her eighties into her nineties, she continued to live a fairly active life. By then, she'd left her Victorian home for a small studio apartment she called her "pad." She regularly walked to the grocery store, maintained a small garden, and fixed her own surprisingly nutritious meals.

And her mind remained as sharp as ever. She could guess the prices on *The Price is Right* and enjoyed following Oregon Ducks basketball on television. Everyone marveled at how gracefully she grew old. She was an inspiration.

But one spring, when she was ninety-two, Grandma fell and broke her pelvis bone. Unable to return to her little "pad," she needed a place to recover. I gladly took her into our home, where my husband, our two preteen sons, and I cared for her. The doctor warned that someone of Grandma's age—and with a heart condition—would in all likelihood not recover. So, realizing she was probably facing the end of her earthly life, my old concerns for her spiritual condition were reawakened.

During this time, Grandma and I had a number of discussions about life and death and heaven, but she made it clear her faith was "personal" to her. I know she had concerns about loved ones who'd previously passed, including her son who tragically drowned as a young man. She was worried about them and not that comfortable talking about it. Looking back, I'm embarrassed to admit her resistance could've been related to my overly zealous enthusiasm. She was glad I began to pursue writing, and reading some of my pieces to her provided a new avenue for more comfortable conversations.

I remember finding Grandma outside in her wheelchair one day that autumn. She was rolling back and forth and singing *How Great Thou Art* under the orange and gold leaves of our giant locust tree. "Doesn't that look just like stained glass?" she happily declared, pointing to the sunlight filtering through the colorful autumn foliage. "Better than any church cathedral."

I had to agree. God's creation was far better than a manmade cathedral. I honestly think that is the point where I set aside my concerns for Grandma's spiritual condition. She was working out her own salvation.

As fall progressed into winter, Grandma's weak heart began to trouble her. Not long after Christmas, she was hospitalized with a severe heart attack. The loss of blood flow and oxygen left her in a coma from which the doctor said she would never recover. We were informed it was time to say our final farewells. As our family tearfully gathered in her hospital room, awkwardly surrounding her bed, it was difficult to say goodbye—mostly because it seemed she was already gone. We felt we were too late. And we were all grieving the loss.

As we stood, encircling Grandma's hospital bed, we began to quietly talk about what a profound influence she'd had on all our lives—this was a truly beloved woman and we would all miss her in our individual ways. We continued to talk, reminiscing over times we'd gathered in her home for holidays. How she could welcome up to twenty relatives into her home, making up extra beds in the barn and the camper, then cooking up a feast for everyone. She was the glue that held the family together. As we talked about her, it was almost as if we were having her memorial service right there.

Suddenly, *Grandma opened her eyes!* Her expression completely stunned us. Her previously faded-gray eyes now looked bright and blue, sparkling with incredible joy. The wide smile spread across her face was equally startling. It was unworldly and bigger than any smile we'd ever seen on her before. It honestly looked as if she'd just seen something miraculous, something far beyond this earth. It really seemed as if she experienced a piece of Heaven—as if she'd just been singing with the angels.

All of us in that room—believers and otherwise—felt something truly amazing happened. So much so we were all speechless at first. We all just stood there staring down into her luminous face—it was almost as if we were getting a tiny glimpse into Heaven. Finally, we began to talk to her, awkwardly asking about where she'd been and what she had seen. And it was obvious she couldn't wait to tell us all about it.

But Grandma was unable to speak. Her words jumbled together like happy baby babbles. And yet, she continued to smile at everyone with an amazing spiritual energy that just seemed to radiate from her. It was unlike anything I've ever seen. After a bit, she seemed to realize her inability to communicate verbally with her loved ones. She simply locked eyes with each of us, one at a time, nodding eagerly and happily—as if trying to share something of vital and joyful importance.

I felt certain she'd just experienced Heaven and wanted us to know all about it. It just seemed obvious. Some members of the family felt this was a sign she was better, that she would recover and go home in a few days. After all, she recovered from having a large tumor removed a few years before. And she nearly recovered from her broken pelvis. Perhaps she would live to be a hundred after all. If anyone could do it, Grandma could.

When the nurses informed us it was time to let her rest, we left feeling encouraged and hopeful. Grandma was okay. And, sure enough, her health did seem to improve throughout the day. But toward that evening, her spirits seemed to lag somewhat. Although she still couldn't speak much, it seemed she was disappointed or dismayed or just plain weary. I honestly think she was simply missing Heaven. I think she said her goodbyes to her family down here and was ready to go join her family up there. For some reason, she was still stuck down here.

As usual, I prayed for Grandma before going to sleep that night. I was no longer worried about her "spiritual condition," I simply wanted God's best for her. Whether she needed to continue her earthly life here or move on to something grander. I felt completely at peace about it. Grandma was okay.

Something woke me early the next morning. It wasn't even 7:00 a.m. yet, and although it wasn't a school day, I got up anyway. I could hear something—tinkling notes coming from the other side of the house. I followed what sounded like a music box playing. Curious as to where this was coming from, I traced the melody to the den—and to the fireplace mantel, which was still decorated for Christmas.

There, in the center of the mantel was a porcelain sculpture I had purchased a few years earlier from a "damaged" table in a pricey little shop. Although the delicate figures of several angels clustered around Baby Jesus in the manger were undamaged and beautiful, the music box beneath them had never worked—which was why it was marked down in the first place. I'd still loved the pretty piece and enjoyed setting it out at Christmastime. I completely forgot about the broken music box hidden in its base.

As I stood there in my nightgown, staring in wonder at the slowly revolving piece sweetly playing "Angels We Have Heard on High," I couldn't quite believe it. How on earth did this happen? No one else was up. The music box was always impossible to wind, and it had never worked before. How odd.

Just then I felt a strange rush go past me. It honestly felt like the rush of angels' wings—although I cannot explain why because I'd never felt anything like that before. But it felt heavenly—and sweet.

I went to the window next to the fireplace. Outside, the sun was just starting to rise, casting golden light. I looked past the leafless locust tree and across a wide field—gazing southward, in the direction of the hospital—and I just knew Grandma was on her way. I knew she was being transported by the angels, going to that place she'd barely visited the day before.

I later learned Grandma peacefully passed away before 7:00 a.m. that morning. I wasn't surprised. Although I was naturally saddened to temporarily lose the sweet woman who was such a blessing in my life, I was glad she was in Heaven—and we would meet again.

And that angelic Christmas figurine? Well, the music box has remained broken—and never played again.

With around 250 books published and 7.5 million sold, **Melody Carlson** is one of the most prolific writers of her generation. Writing primarily for women and teens, and in various genres, she has won numerous national awards—including the Rita, Gold Medallion, Carol Award, and two career achievement awards. Melody and her husband live in the Pacific Northwest.

ANGEL GLIMPSES

However poor a preacher, I can preach the gospel better than Gabriel can, because Gabriel cannot say what I can say: "I am a sinner saved by grace."

—A. T. Pierson[19]

CHAPTER THIRTEEN

ANGELS UNAWARE

SARENA WELLMAN

I n 1997, I had just turned nineteen. I had an important decision to make about whether to join a team from my church going on a mission trip to Russia. I had been involved in a short-term mission trip to Jamaica the previous spring, and I was hesitant to ask my friends and family for money to support another trip only two months later.

Nevertheless, my pastor, Dr. Carl Diemer, and his wife, Dr. Carolyn Diemer, relentlessly urged me to go. Carolyn wrote a children's book, titled *What the Bible Teaches About Life After Death*, that was translated into the Russian language. The purpose of the trip was to distribute the book and, ultimately, the Gospel to some unreached groups in Russia.

I decided that if God wanted me to go, He would provide the financial support. In other words, if any money came in, it would be a sign God wanted me to be part of this trip.

On March 23, the first Sunday I announced I might be going, someone gave me money. I can't remember who or how much, but it wasn't more than a hundred dollars. The cost of the trip was going to be more than twenty-four hundred. Remaining faithful to my promise, I committed to going.

PREPARATION

At that time, passports were not required to fly to Jamaica, which was the only country I had ever visited. Not only would a passport be required for a trip to Russia, but a visa as well.

I began the tedious process of applying for a passport. We were to leave for Russia on Monday, May 12, with Revival Fires Ministries, a mission organization out of Branson, Missouri. The trip was six weeks away, and the passport was supposed to arrive in four to six weeks. I would be cutting it close.

Four weeks passed. Support money was rolling in. I was nearly at my goal, but my passport had not yet arrived. My father and mother, Walter and Karen Beasley, were my rocks through the whole ordeal. My mother called the passport office to see if there was any way they could rush it. They said it should arrive in time for my trip.

"We will just pray the passport will arrive in time to get your visa," my parents said.

I lived in a small rural town called Evington—I'm not even sure if it qualified as a town. The post office was so tiny, incoming mail was delivered twenty-four to forty-eight hours after it arrived in the office. We learned, however, we could pick up packages from the post office when they arrived. Beginning about two weeks prior to the trip, I called the post office every day to see if my passport arrived. The lady who worked there came to know my voice. The conversation would go like this:

"Hi, I'm calling to see if—"

"No, Sarena. I'm sorry, dear. It hasn't arrived yet," the post office lady would cut me off in reply.

We were leaving on May 12. On May 9 when I called the post office, the lady had good news.

"Hi, it's Sarena."

"It came! It came!"

I jumped in the car and drove to the post office to retrieve my precious package.

I called Revival Fires, and my contact, Linda, told me what to do next. I contacted the visa office in Washington, D.C., and faxed them a copy of my passport.

"Our office is closed tomorrow [Saturday], and it will take an entire day to process the visa. We will not be able to have the visa ready until Tuesday," the woman at the help desk explained.

My heart sank. I would not be able to travel with my team. I went ahead and arranged for the visa to be overnighted to JFK Airport on Tuesday and called Linda again.

"Linda, I have bad news. My visa will not be ready until Tuesday."

Linda searched her database to find a solution to the problem.

"Praise God! We have a group of three women leaving from JFK Tuesday evening at 6:00 p.m. That will give your visa plenty of time to arrive in New York!"

At least I would not have to travel alone.

On Monday, May 12, I said farewell to my pastor and the rest of our team, letting them know I would meet them in Rome on Wednesday morning before they left for Moscow. I packed and weighed my two allowed suitcases. I was taking one old beat-up suitcase that held a fax machine we were taking to a Russian church. I padded the fax machine with plenty of old T-shirts I intended to give away. I did not plan to bring the suitcase or any of its contents back with me.

My other suitcase held all my clothes, toiletries, and a few extra items like candy and cards. In my backpack, I packed a change of clothes and some toiletries.

After packing, I was so tired I lay down for a short nap. That nap ended up lasting four hours, so when bedtime arrived Monday evening, I couldn't sleep. I lay awake almost all night in anticipation of the drive to New York the next morning.

Morning finally came. My sister, Kristi, and my mother were driving me to JFK. We left early Tuesday and arrived in New York at 2:00 p.m. My visa was supposed to arrive at noon. After reaching the airport, I checked my bags and received my boarding pass. Then we located the gate from which my flight would leave at 6:00 p.m. Next, our little trio located the air cargo area, the place where incoming airmail packages were received and processed. The air cargo department was several floors down and on a different concourse. It took us twenty minutes and a few elevator rides to reach it, but my hopes were high—finally, everything worked out.

When I asked about my visa at the desk, the man working there checked the docket and frowned. "Due to some delays in D.C., the plane carrying your package won't arrive until about four. Sorry."

My heart sank, but what could we do? I swallowed my disappointment and tried to think about something else. My mom kept urging me to have faith; the Lord would work everything out.

At 4:00 p.m., we went back to air cargo. No package. More delays.

After our third trip to air cargo, the older man at the desk said, "Listen, sweetie, I will keep watching the flight schedule. As soon as that visa arrives, I will personally run it up to you. What's your gate?" I told him the gate number, and we went back upstairs.

Could I trust that man to keep his word? Could I trust the Lord to get my visa to me on time?

My flight to Rome started boarding at 5:30 p.m. I had already met the three women with whom I was to travel. I boarded the plane without a visa and with my heart in my throat.

It was 5:45 p.m. Still nothing.

At 5:50 p.m., the flight attendant began walking down the aisle of the cabin, looking at seat numbers. I knew she was coming for me. Her eyes paused on my seat number, then her gaze shifted to me. "I'm sorry, but I'm going to have to ask you to leave the plane," she said. "We cannot let you fly without a visa."

Slowly, I stood. I felt the pressure of dozens of eyes on me. Yes, it was embarrassing, but more than that, I could not understand how God would let this happen. I was certain He wanted me to go on this trip. So why hadn't anything worked out as it should?

God, I prayed as I walked down the aisle, *I don't understand what's going on. But if You want me in Russia, I know You can get me there. I'll trust in You.*

Kristi and Mom were still in the waiting area. Kristi plastered a smile on her face, trying to be strong for me. Mom was crying. I followed Mom's lead.

We sat there while the plane sat outside the gate. The flight attendants closed the door. I looked at that closed door and thought I understood how the people of Noah's time must have felt when God closed the door to the ark.

But this time, I believed God would open another door.

Two minutes after I sat down to wait, the kind gentleman from air cargo came racing through the concourse. His knees were pumping as he ran in the direction of our gate, his necktie flapping behind him. He held up a package as he ran, yelling, "I've got it! I've got it!"

Hope blossomed in my heart. Maybe I could still make this flight!

But the gate attendant shook her head.

"The plane is still sitting right there! Why can't she get on?" the gentleman implored.

"I'm sorry, but they've closed the door and begun the pre-flight checklist. I can't open it," the lady said. "Besides, they've already taken her bags off the plane."

He slammed his fist on the desk. "Well, you need to find a way to get her there!"

The gate attendant smiled. "I'll do my best."

The man walked over to us, still breathless after his sprint through the terminal. He handed me the visa. "I'm sorry. I came as fast as I could."

"That's okay," my sister answered. "It will all work out."

The man stayed with us while the gate attendant typed furiously at her computer. A few minutes later, she gasped, "It's a miracle! But you have to leave *now!*"

The man from air cargo grinned as we sprang into action.

The flight she put me on was several gates away and already boarding. My team would leave Rome the next morning but would stop for a brief layover in Milan, Italy. My new flight would put me in Milan in time to catch up with them. The only hitch was that their plane would be coming into a different airport.

The gate attendant gave me quick instructions about switching airports via bus, but everything was happening so quickly I didn't catch everything she said.

Tears of joy, relief, and sheer terror flowed again, all at once. I had never flown on my own—I'd never traveled farther than a few hours by car on my own. I hugged the gentleman from air cargo, and Mom and Kristi ran with me to the gate. I didn't really have time to think; none of us did. I said goodbye to my sister, who smiled through all the craziness, and then my mother, who was trying to be brave.

With my pulse pounding, I boarded the plane for Milan. *Here we go, Lord. Jesus. Help me through this.*

The Alitalia flight left JFK at approximately 6:45 p.m. I would arrive in Milan early the next morning, around 8:45 a.m. local time.

Time for sleep. I had not slept in more than twenty-four hours, and I was exhausted. But the eight-month-old seated next to me with his mama was not sleepy. He stayed awake the entire flight, and so did I. Eight hours passed. Eight long hours.

Finally, we arrived in Milan. Because I was in the middle seat, I was pretty much the last one off the plane. After entering the airport, I wandered aimlessly looking for a bus station. About the time I spotted a bus icon on an overhead sign, I heard my name over the intercom, "Sarena Beasley, report to the bus station. Sarena Beasley, report to the bus station."

I found the bus station just as my bus was pulling out. The attendant looked at my flight information and told me to get on the next bus, which arrived about ten minutes later. After boarding, I was in good spirits, even though I missed both a flight and a bus. I chatted with a few American tourists and explained my situation. "If you were my daughter, I don't think I could have let you get on that plane," one of the ladies said.

I gave her a confident smile. "Well, God will see me through!"

When the bus stopped, everyone got off. Except me. The bus driver turned to stare at me. "Get off here!"

"But I'm supposed to go to the other airport," I said, certain there was a mistake.

"This bus goes back to the airport you came from," he said, his voice gruff. "You have to get on that bus." He pointed to a bus just ahead.

I got off the bus, but I was too late to catch the other bus. I had to wait for the next one. I was beginning to notice a pattern. I waited about ten minutes for the next bus, wondering how much time I had to make my flight. Once I finally arrived at the airport, I made my way to my assigned gate. *I made it! Thank you, Jesus!*

I was moments away from being reunited with my team. I located the gate and stood in line, glancing out the window and hoping to see my pastor or someone from my team through those tiny airplane windows.

The attendant took my ticket. I was about to step forward and board the jet, but instead, I heard her say, "You cannot get on. The plane is over capacity."

I blinked. "What do you mean?"

The lady was not as nice as the gate attendant in the States. She looked at me without answering, then looked back at her computer as if the answer should be obvious.

To this point, I (mostly) stayed calm with a smile on my face, other than the few tears I shed in New York. I became distraught. I thought God worked everything out, so why weren't things working? Even the gate attendant back at JFK proclaimed my situation a miracle, right? It was seeming less like a miracle with every passing moment.

I took a deep breath and tried to clue her in to the miracle she was missing. "You don't understand! I was supposed to meet my group here. They are on that plane. I have to get on."

She sighed and rolled her eyes.

"Can't you at least let me on for a minute so they can know I'm here?"

She sighed again. "No."

Tears filled my eyes. "Can you get someone to take them a note at least?"

"No," she said more forcefully. Clearly, she saw me as a nuisance. "Here's your new flight schedule. You will fly to Paris, then make a connection to Moscow, Russia. Your plane will arrive at 11:00 p.m. local time."

She dismissed me with a gesture to move aside. I stepped out of the way, feeling like I couldn't breathe. I was trying to hold it together, but nothing made sense. Why would God bring me all this way and have me miss yet another flight? As soon as everything seemed like it was going to be okay, it wasn't.

I made my way to the lower level of the airport and located my gate. As I arrived, I saw a man running out to a bus to get to the flight. I hurried to the door and held out my boarding pass. The gate attendants stopped me.

"I have to get on that flight!" I shrieked, fighting back tears.

"This is not your flight," one of them told me in broken English. She rolled her eyes and told me to sit down—my plane was not yet boarding. They spoke to each other in Italian and laughed, looking in my direction. That only made my tears flow more freely, except now they were tears of anger and frustration. *God, what are You doing?*

My faith began to waver. Disappointment, frustration, and exhaustion set in. The confident girl from the first bus ride had begun to disappear.

About half an hour later, the flight began to board for Paris, France. I lost all track of time. I don't even think I was wearing a watch. Even so, it probably wasn't correct. I had mostly put my emotions in check, but my bleary red eyes gave me away.

"Are you afraid to fly?" The words came from a French flight attendant in her thirties. She knew I was upset.

I swallowed the lump in my throat and nodded. The sympathetic look on her face nearly brought on another wave of tears.

"This is what I take when I'm afraid," she said, producing a few white capsules from her pocket.

My eyes widened. "Oh no! I'm not afraid of flying. I'm afraid of what will happen when I get there."

She finished boarding the passengers, then came to find me. She asked me to explain my worries. My whole story came spilling out—the missed flights, the lack of sleep, and how I had no idea how to navigate the Paris airport.

"I'm so sorry," she said. "Let me see what I can do to help."

She returned a few moments later and helped me move to an empty row. "Once the plane has reached cruising altitude, you can lie down," she said. "These other seats are empty."

After we were airborne, I did lie down. It had been about forty hours since I last slept well. I didn't sleep long, but I did get about thirty minutes of deep sleep before dinner was served. The flight attendant slipped me a few extra rolls, about the only edible part of the meal. I slept another half an hour or so after the dinner trays were taken away.

Then I heard my name. The flight attendant was standing beside me.

"I checked the flight schedules of the other passengers. There are three women who are making the same connecting flight as you. I spoke to them, and they have agreed to help you through the Paris airport."

"Thank you so much," I said, tears threatening to spill again.

Each time I started to despair, God offered a little calm in the midst of the never-ending storm. That three-hour flight did a world of good to my tired spirit.

Thank you, Jesus, for the kind flight attendant and the women who will help me. Before leaving the plane, I thanked the flight attendant for her kindness.

The Paris airport was a nightmare. I walked as fast as I could, but it seemed to take forever to reach the appropriate gate. I felt like a small child following those women through the massive space. Two of the women spoke English. They left me to go grab some dinner. They asked if I wanted to come, but given my record of missing flights, I decided to stay put at the gate.

After about an hour layover, our flight to Moscow was ready to board. It was to arrive in Moscow at approximately 11:00 p.m. My seat on the flight happened to be next to the woman who did not speak English. She was traveling with a young child and was mostly preoccupied throughout the flight. Had she been able to speak English, I doubt she would have had much to say. My cheerful spirit was renewed, although I was reluctant to get my hopes up too high. I was finally headed to Moscow.

As we neared the airport, the flight attendant passed out customs reports. I took mine and stared at the Russian text.

My flying buddy turned the form over for me. English. Phew!

I filled out my first customs report ever. On the line marked, "Drugs," I began listing all of the over-the-counter medications I brought, such as Tylenol, Advil, etc.

My new friend snatched the customs report from me and pointed to the section. "No!" she said emphatically. She crumpled up the form and asked for another. This time she pointed to the "drugs" section and said, "No," again.

I checked "None."

When we disembarked in Moscow, I searched for the other two women. We met on the way through the terminal. Before we reached customs, however, the two English-speaking women went through a different gate because of a work visa. I was stuck with the woman who didn't speak English at all. Well, except for the word *no*.

I followed her through customs. I'm fairly certain I held my breath as the guard looked over my customs form. I breathed a sigh of relief as he allowed me to pass.

Almost there!

I followed the lady to baggage claim. Bag after bag came up, but only the old blue suitcase containing the fax machine arrived. I glanced around and saw the airport was fairly empty. I didn't recognize anyone. No one held up a sign with my name on it. Nobody even remotely looked as if he were searching for someone. The passengers from my flight were leaving.

Had I made it to Moscow only to spend the night in the airport? *How much worse can this get?*

Exasperated, I went to the nearest desk to explain my bag was missing, along with my ride. Riding a coaster of emotions and exhausted from a lack of sleep, I had difficulty reigning in my emotions. My voice cracked and tears leaked from my eyes no matter how hard I tried to restrain them. Nobody seemed to understand my situation. To be fair, even those who might have spoken English probably could not have understood me with my wobbly voice. I was about to lose it.

Suddenly, the woman from the plane approached with a man who seemed to know a few phrases in English. I didn't even realize she was still at the airport. She patted my arm and said something in Russian, then walked away. I assumed she was telling me she had to go. It was 11:30 p.m.

"Do you speak English?" The man asked, his accent thick and heavy.

I nodded.

"Spanish?" he asked again.

I hesitated. I took Spanish in high school for two years. But I probably had a better chance of understanding Spanish than Russian. I nodded again.

The man's face lit up. "Ahh, Spanish," he said. "Wait here."

Great. Just great. Now I would have to attempt to recall the eight phrases in Spanish I remembered. I struggled to remember the words for "suitcase" or "bag" or "desolate" until the man returned with another man in tow.

The new arrival nodded as the first man explained something in Russian. He looked at me and smiled in a kindly expression I had not seen since the attendant on the Paris flight. I braced myself, fully expecting a Spanish phrase to come from his lips.

"How can I help you?" he asked in slightly broken English.

All my emotions flooded out. I nearly hugged the guy. I managed to choke out my primary problems. "One of my bags is missing, nobody is here to pick me up, and I have no idea where my team is," I explained without taking a breath.

He smiled again. "Come with me."

I followed him to a desk near the baggage claim. He spoke to the people there and translated their response, "They say you should come back in the morning. Since you changed planes so many times, your bag may just be delayed a bit."

"Okay, what about my team? I have no idea where they are. Someone was supposed to be here to pick me up from the airport.

And everything happened so quickly, I have no contact information for anyone here."

The gentleman with blue eyes reminded me a bit of the kind cargo clerk from JFK. I noticed his nametag. I don't remember the name or whether it was written in English or Russian. I assume it would have been Russian, but many of the letters in the Cyrillic alphabet make the same sound as English letters. My pastor was taking Russian classes, so he taught me the sounds of the letters that were different. I do remember it was not an ordinary name for a Russian such as Demetri or Sergei, but something simple, like Tomas.

Tomas again asked me to follow him. "There are pay phones upstairs. You can use one to call somebody."

Tomas walked to the desk in the phone station. I had not yet exchanged any American dollars for rubles, so Tomas paid for me to use the phone. I later learned the cost of the three-minute phone call was equivalent to about twenty-one American dollars.

It was 11:45 p.m. Moscow time, 9:45 a.m. Eastern Standard Time when I called my mother.

"Mom?"

"Sarena! It's so good to hear your voice!" Instant tears.

I tried desperately to rein in my emotions. "Mom, I only have three minutes."

"Honey, what's wrong?"

"I'm in Moscow at the airport, but there's nobody here to pick me up and I have no idea where to go."

"Oh, dear. This is what I was dreading. They must think you are coming tomorrow." Mom paused. "Listen, you stay right where you are. I'll call Linda at Revival Fires and let her know the situation. Is there a number on this phone so I can call you back?"

I read her the number from the pay phone and we hung up.

Tomas tapped me lightly on the shoulder. "You have to leave now," he said, smiling.

"What? I can't leave now! My mom is calling me back on this phone!"

"It is nearly midnight. The airport is closing. You must leave now. The last taxi is coming." He nodded. "I will stay to tell your mother where you are."

I reluctantly followed Tomas down the stairs. He showed me a list of hotels. I saw *Novotel* and vaguely remembered my pastor's wife talking about that hotel in one of our meetings.

"Novotel." I pointed. "I remember someone talking about the Novotel!" *Please let them be there!*

"Ah! The Novotel." Tomas seemed pleased. He took me outside to the curb and told me to wait for the Novotel taxi to arrive. "Do not worry! I will go back to tell your mother where you are."

And with that, he was gone.

I stood on the curb in the dark. It was midnight in Moscow. I just trusted a total stranger to call me a cab and also to relay my whereabouts to the only other person on the planet who knew I was no longer in America.

I was on the lowest level of the airport. I remember an overhang blocking most of the light. To my right, two older men spoke in low tones. They started to approach me. *Lord, where is Tomas? Why did he leave me here? Please protect me!*

On the inside, I was shaking, but on the outside, I stood perfectly still. The men came closer and asked me something in Russian. I understood the word *taxi* and relaxed a bit. I replied in Russian, "Nyet."

They moved on. *Thank You, Jesus!*

A few minutes later, the taxi arrived and I got in. The driver took me to a huge hotel practically across the street from the airport. I approached the front desk and asked if they had received any phone calls. The desk clerk looked confused. He was a younger gentleman, probably in his early twenties. "Nobody has called in the past ten minutes at least," he said.

"My mother is supposed to call me here. Do you mind if I wait on the couch over there?" I asked.

At that point, the humor in the situation struck me. I was asking to lie down on a couch in the lobby of a four-star hotel. I imagine I appeared pretty ragged.

The desk clerk nodded his approval. Who knows what he was thinking about the crazy American?

I dozed on the couch until the desk clerk came to tap my shoulder. He told me I had a phone call.

I answered the phone.

"Sarena?" My mom sounded a bit desperate.

"Yes, Mom. It's me." Tears sprang to my eyes again at the sound of her voice. Tomas had kept his promise.

"Oh, my goodness! I was so worried! I called the number you gave me and some man told me to call this number. I'm so glad you're okay! Stay there. Chuck is on his way to pick you up at the airport. I have to call Linda back to let her know you aren't there anymore."

"I won't go anywhere this time, Mom!" She hung up.

Some of my worry faded. Chuck Todd was the leader of Revival Fires Missions. He was married to a Russian woman, Helen, which (I believe) gave him citizenship in Russia and America. If Chuck knew I was in Russia, I was going to be fine.

I walked over to the desk clerk and explained that someone was coming to pick me up at the airport, but now my mother had to tell them I was at the hotel. He nodded. Although his English was impressive, I didn't know how much he understood. At the time, I didn't really care. I was exhausted and close to being able to finally sleep. I returned to the couch and laid down again.

The desk clerk tapped me a few moments later. "You have *two* phone calls," he said, holding up two fingers.

I blinked and wondered who else would be calling. "Two?" He nodded.

I followed him back to the front desk and answered one of the phones.

"Hello?"

"Hi, honey. It's me," Mom said. "I called Linda, and she said she was going to call Chuck to have him pick you up from the Novotel instead."

"I have another phone call on the other line," I explained. "That might be him. Hold on."

I told the desk clerk to connect me to the other phone call. "Hello?"

"Hi, Sarena. This is Chuck Todd. How are you?" The genuine concern in his voice caused the tears to start again. I no longer had any control over my emotions.

"I'm fine," I answered, not trusting my voice to say more.

"I am so sorry. We checked all the flight records, but there was no record of your arrival. But you did the right thing going to the Novotel. Listen, you've been through a lot. You get a room there tonight. You will be safe. You need sleep," he said. "Besides, there's no way to get you to your team until tomorrow. They are four hours away."

"Okay," I answered.

He explained a few more details, and we said our goodbyes.

I relayed the information to my mother, and she reluctantly agreed that I should be fine. She had not felt right about letting me get on the plane in the first place but told herself I would be okay once I reached Moscow.

"I'll be fine, Mom," I said. "Chuck said it was very safe."

"Okay. I'll call you in half an hour to be sure you got into your room. Don't open the door to anyone."

"I won't, Mom," I reassured her. "I'll be fine."

I just spent nearly half an hour sleeping on the couch in the lobby. I was not worried about security. I hung up and told the desk clerk I needed a room.

He looked puzzled. "I thought someone was coming to pick you up."

"I thought so, too," I answered. "But now they are coming in the morning."

"Okay," he answered. He told me the price of the room in rubles.

"Umm—I don't have any rubles," I answered. "Do you take dollars?"

"No, you will have to exchange."

"Where can I exchange money at one in the morning?" I teetered on the edge of a breakdown.

The desk clerk calmly pointed behind me. I turned to see a giant sign declaring, *Exchange* in neon letters. How did I miss that? This had to be the most patient desk clerk ever.

I crossed the lobby and exchanged all my money to rubles. I had slightly more than enough for the room, which was over $200 American for the night. I don't remember why I was carrying so much money with me, but I guess it was because God knew I would need it.

I entered my room on the third floor. I found Jay Leno on television, the only show I could find in English, and waited for my mother to call. I did not have to wait long. "Hello?"

"Hi, honey. Are you okay?"

"Yes, Mom. I'm fine. I'm exhausted."

"I bet! Well, you sleep, and I'll keep in contact with Linda on my end. She'll let me know when you reach the rest of your team."

Shortly after we hung up, the phone rang again.

"Sarena?" The voice was male and heavily accented.

Too tired to think, I answered, "Yes?"

"What are you doing tomorrow?"

I paused. Who was calling me? The desk clerk, maybe? Perhaps he wanted to know when I would be checking out? I was not thinking clearly, so I answered, "Chuck said he would pick me up in the morning."

"Oh! You talk to Chuck?"

"Yes."

"Oh! Okay," he answered. "I see you tomorrow."

I hung up, confused. I should have asked who was calling. Too late now.

I turned the deadbolt on the door and fell asleep almost as soon as I hit the bed.

WEDNESDAY, MAY 14

I awoke at 10 a.m. I slept for eight hours and was still tired. I showered and collected my things. I slept through breakfast but figured we would probably eat soon because it was nearly noon. I hadn't eaten anything since the flight to Moscow twelve hours earlier.

When I reached the lobby, Chuck Todd was waiting for me along with a young man, Igor, who was about my age. Igor was the man who called the night before. He was going to travel with me to meet my group. He was my interpreter for the day.

Chuck reimbursed me for the cost of the hotel room and asked about my trip. I briefly explained the whole fiasco in JFK and how I missed the connection in Milan.

"No wonder there was no record of your flights!" he said. "But how did you get to the Novotel?"

I relayed the story of the airport to him, telling how thoughtful and nice Tomas had been and how he paid for my phone call.

"Wow! That's unheard of around here," Chuck said. "We need to pay that man back and go check on your luggage."

A few moments later, Igor and I walked across to the airport. Chuck gave us enough money to cover the cost of the phone call as well as a bit extra. We were going to reimburse the man and check on the status of my bag.

We checked the baggage claim desk first with no luck. Then we asked to speak to Tomas.

"Nobody by that name works here," Igor interpreted.

"Do they understand that we want to give him money? That I am not upset with him?" I asked.

Igor spoke again, then turned back to me. "He says nobody by that name works here," he said again.

"Can we ask to speak to a manager?"

Igor relayed the information, and we were directed to a different area. Igor explained the situation again and asked for Tomas by name.

"The manager says nobody works here by that name. Can you explain what he looked like?" Igor asked.

I gave a description of his approximate height, hair color, eye color, and what he was wearing. Igor interpreted. The manager checked the schedule of who was there the night before, then looked at me and shook his head. He spoke briefly to Igor, who ended the conversation and thanked the manager before turning back to me.

"He says nobody was working here last night by that name or description." He shrugged. "It's a miracle!"

I stood in silence, dazed. I could not believe it at first. Igor's immediate conclusion of this being a miracle pricked my heart. I had questioned God several times over the past three days. I knew He wanted me in Russia. I knew it because, from the beginning, He provided the way and the means. But the trip was so difficult, and I couldn't understand the purpose for the bumps along the way.

Now it became clear. Without the hardships, there would be no room for miracles.

Thank You, Father, for taking care of me. And forgive my faltering faith. I know You brought me here for Your purpose. Help me be a witness for You!

We walked in silence back to the hotel. Chuck was still there, finalizing plans for the day. I relayed the scenario to him. He was amazed as well. "God is good!" he exclaimed.

REUNION

Igor and I traveled with a van driver to Kaluga, Russia, a small town about four hours south of Moscow. Although we left at noon, we did not arrive until after dark because we had to stop at a warehouse at the opposite end of Moscow to pick up books needed for the trip. Igor stopped at a kiosk to buy four cans of Coca-Cola, two for him and two for me. We drank one right away as we began our trek. We did not stop for lunch.

After spending eight hours in a small van, Igor and I became fast friends. I learned quite a bit about our driver as well. I helped load the books at the warehouse. I shared a package of Snickers miniatures I had in my bag. Finally, we reached Kaluga.

We drove from hotel to hotel. At each stop, Igor went in and ask if any Americans were staying there. If so, he asked how many. When he finally heard the correct number, we waited in the lobby to see if my team would arrive. Igor and I drank hot tea. I didn't even like hot tea. But it was something.

Finally, my team arrived. When Dr. Diemer walked in, he nearly teared up. "Sarena! You made it!" He hugged me tightly. "Don't you ever do that to me again!!"

"Believe me, I won't!" I laughed. The team gathered around in the lobby to hear about my little adventure. I told them about Tomas and all the others who helped me along the way. One of the team members asked, "Did it ever occur to you that maybe God didn't want you to come?"

"No," I answered truthfully. "That never crossed my mind."

"Why not?"

"Simple," I said. "If God didn't want me here, I wouldn't be here. If anyone didn't want me here, it's the devil."

"I'm so glad you are here!" Another team member said. "I was going to lead the music tonight because you weren't here. Now you can do it!"

"Sure!" I agreed, ready to get to work. I had missed an entire day.

THURSDAY, MAY 15

The next evening, our team arrived at the theater that had held twenty-five kids the night before. But those twenty-five each invited ten of their closest friends. The auditorium held roughly 250 people, mostly children.

I led the children in several well-known American children's songs. I smile to think a small population in Kaluga, Russia, probably still knows the English words and motions to "Who Is the King of the Jungle?" and "Hallelu, Hallelu," as well as several other children's songs.

Other members of our team put on puppet shows and preached the Gospel. We distributed Bibles and copies of Dr. Carolyn Diemer's books. Because few Americans visited that area, the children thought we were famous. Every night, they bombarded us with requests to autograph their books.

During the day, we visited orphanages, hospitals, and homes for the elderly to pass out Bibles and books as well. All in all, we probably distributed a few thousand books during those ten days. I was amazed to see how hungry those people were to learn about God.

This side of Heaven, I will never know for certain if Tomas was an angel sent by God to intervene for me, but I believe he was. What would have happened had Tomas not been there? Angel or not, God *did* ordain for Tomas to be there at that specific time. In fact, throughout my entire travel ordeal, I was never out of His care.

Perhaps I met other angels along the way—the man who ran headlong through the airport to bring me my visa and insisted on waiting with me until arrangements were made to reach my group.

The flight attendant who took it upon herself to check every other passenger's connecting flight so I would not be alone in Paris.

The non–English speaking woman who kept me from being detained or arrested upon entering the country and was responsible for finding Tomas in the first place.

They could have all been angels.

But in any case, I praise God for watching over me and sending people to keep a young, inexperienced woman safe and sane. And one day in eternity, I may meet people from Russia who came to know Christ because of the Gospel message my team and I helped spread among those wonderful people.

Sarena Wellman resides in Lynchburg, Virginia, with her husband, Greg, and two boys, Levi and Jude. Since the first trip to Russia, she developed a love of mission work, especially for the Russian people, and traveled to Russian-speaking countries on four other occasions. She teaches at a local public middle school and remains very active in her church and community. She hopes to one day return to mission work.

ANGEL GLIMPSES

The Relationship Between Angels and Stars

Many times, when the Hebrew word for *stars* is used, the Old Testament writers implied that they are more than astronomical entities. They speak of stars in more personal ways; the stars are said to fight, sing, and even err (Judg. 5:20; Job 15:15, 25:5, 38:7, Ps. 148:3).

Also, the New Testament gives evidence of some relationship between stars and angels. The Greek word for *stars* often denotes or symbolizes a personal entity (e.g., 1 Cor. 15:35–45; Jude 13) and not just a heavenly luminary. Christ Himself is called "the morning star" (2 Pet. 1:19; Rev. 22:16). The "star" that led the Magi to the Christ child is believed by some to be the Shekinah glory of God, thereby indicating the Lord was present among men.[20]

What then is the relationship between angels and stars? James Woychuck's summary seems to fit the biblical picture:

> Biblical testimony does not remove all the mystery from the connection between the stars and angels. The exact relationship of stars and angels may be inconceivable and inexpressible this side of Heaven. But God's Word does reveal that, by God's design, the countless millions of stars visually portray the countless millions of angels. Further, this portrayal extends to depict a presently indefinable intersection in the being of stars and angels. Therefore, the stars do not merely offer an illustration of the innumerable and powerful angels but also portray God's vast armies of light intentionally, creatively, and universally. When people look up on a twinkling gust of shining diamonds too numerous to count, they see the visual representation of the angels. They see stars and yet, in a mysterious way, they see something more.[21,22]

GO HOME? DON'T HAVE TO TELL ME TWICE!

JENNIFER L. PORTER

BOB

"Pay attention to the road! Stay in your own lane!" His hand hovered over the horn as he glanced at the car beside him. He felt his anger rising as his stomach rumbled. Had he eaten today? He couldn't remember, except maybe a donut and a cup of coffee. His mouth dropped open as one hand rose from the steering wheel.

"Really, lady, who puts on mascara while driving?" He shook his head and merged into the right lane. "Might as well shove a toothpick in your eye!"

The San Mateo exit lay ahead, so he flipped on his turn signal. San Francisco, California, was a beautiful city if you were fortunate enough to be strolling along Fisherman's Wharf or picnicking in the park near the Golden Gate Bridge. But here, in bumper-to-bumper traffic, San Francisco looked like any other unending freeway.

"Hate traffic, hate traffic—no, I *despise* traffic." The word left his lips in a hiss. He never planned to move his young family to a rapidly growing metropolis, but he and his wife discussed it, and she said she'd follow him anywhere. Moving felt like the beginning of a new adventure.

Two weeks later, he and his wife, Jenn, pulled up stakes and moved their family from Wilmington, Delaware, to Phoenix, Arizona. Now, they and their three boys lived in Scottsdale, Arizona, and he was traveling on business, stuck once again in San Francisco traffic.

His business cards tucked in the cup holder read, "Bob Porter, Vice President."

For nearly a year, he'd been a vice president for a medical recruitment company in Phoenix. Was it worth it? A vision of his new house flashed through his mind. The benefits were excellent, allowing him to pay for his wife's mounting medical bills. Discovering she had Lyme disease was almost a relief after a year and a half of constant fevers and swollen joints. But the latest treatment failed. She was weaker every day.

He hated leaving her—well, everyone—so that's why he paid for her grandmother to come stay while he was away on business.

"Go home!"

He swerved when the voice spoke behind him. "What the—?"

He glanced at the radio—it was off—then looked over his shoulder into the back seat.

No stowaway; he was alone in the car. But who said that? People who heard voices were hidden away in mental asylums, and rightfully so.

Dude, he told himself, *you really need to get some sleep.*

Another quick glance into his rearview mirror assured him the voice must have been his imagination, but a shiver ran down his spine—along with an increasing desire to hurry home.

His stomach growled, and logic took over. Going on to Phoenix was suicidal. He could be at his hotel in forty minutes, enjoying room service, and a nice juicy steak.

His mouth watered at the notion of real food. The thought of changing out of his suit and into shorts and a T-shirt was also appealing. The hotel was already booked. But he heard that voice . . .

He pulled in a deep breath. "Yep, going home now." At least he was going to make a Herculean effort to get there. The hotel amenities sounded great, but he'd rather be home. Some guys stayed on the road every day they could, but he was not that man.

But what about that voice? Could it have been some kind of angelic warning? He did believe angels were God's messengers, but he didn't believe in the Barbie/Tinkerbell variety with cotton-candy hair and glow-in-the-dark wings. The current cultural angel mania kept him from talking about the day he should have died.

Six years earlier, Bob and Jenn had belonged to a Bible study group that gathered at an old home set on a hill, with concrete steps rising from the the sidewalk to the porch. One evening, when the group was chatting on the porch, Bob fell backward and was about to strike the back of his head on the cement steps. His wife watched in horror and screamed just before his neck made contact. She later told him she knew she was about to become a widow.

Then, without a logical or scientific explanation, his body went vertical, and he found himself on his feet. Everyone started cheering as he ran back up the steps. Being a natural joker, he slapped his forehead like Curly from *The Three Stooges* and yelled, "Woo, woo, woo, woo!"

One of the women sang out Amy Grant's "Angels Watching Over Me."

He knew he had experienced a miracle, but being a naturally private man, he kept it to himself.

Now, nearly thirty-four years later, he could still feel the hands that saved him. They were strong and lifted him onto his feet as if he were a small child.

Maybe something like that had just happened again. After all, it wasn't every day he heard voices in the back seat.

A detailed plan began to form in his head. Going home would add another four hours to his day, but he was willing to attempt it.

Hotels had long since lost their allure. His wife enjoyed staying in hotels, but he would always rather sleep in his own bed. So, by hook or by crook he was going to take a shot. If he didn't catch his flight, he'd know going home wasn't meant to be.

He merged into the traffic heading toward San Francisco International Airport. If he could make it to the airport and get a seat on the 8:30 p.m. flight, he could be home before midnight.

But everything would have to line up perfectly if he was going to make it home.

When he got to the airport, he dropped off his rental car and ran toward the terminal. Because this was before the heightened security of the post-9/11 era, the airport attendants nearly waved him through to his gate. His preoccupation with getting home was growing stronger, and as he offered his license and credit card to the woman at the ticket counter, he didn't care how much the ticket cost. He was going home no matter what.

The attendant smiled. "Lucky man, you got the last flight out to Phoenix." With monsoon rains rolling in, all later flights would be delayed. "They're boarding now, so you're going to have to hoof it if you want to get on that plane."

Bob thanked the woman and took off. He was a good athlete, but the run left him breathless as he sprinted through the airport in his dress suit and stiff shoes, a heavy briefcase in one hand and a duffle strapped across his back. Finally, breathless and perspiring, he boarded the plane just before the flight attendants closed the doors.

He nodded to the flight attendant and lowered his hands to his knees to catch his breath. His lungs were burning. When he could breathe, he walked down the aisle, noticing the plane was filled except for one middle seat. Great. They'd need a shoe horn to pry him out later.

"Please take your seats." After shoving his duffle in the overhead compartment, Bob squeezed himself into the empty middle seat and fastened the seat belt. Although he'd lost some of his girth since playing college football, his six-foot-four-inch frame did not take kindly to being squeezed into small spaces. His knees hit the seat back in front of him, and he had to hunch his shoulders forward to keep his arms from invading the space of the people sitting next to him. This wasn't going to be a comfortable flight, but at least he'd made it.

He allowed himself to breathe. Good. Mission accomplished. He'd be home around midnight, so he'd just close his eyes and try to make the best of it.

The plane hit a few pockets of turbulence but landed smoothly at Phoenix International Airport.

A storm hit as he drove home. Rain blurred his vision as raindrops spattered the windshield and lightning flashed on the horizon. He switched on the wipers and headed north.

He pulled into the driveway and sighed in relief—the house was still standing. He entered quietly through the laundry room, not wanting to wake anyone. No toys littered the floor because Jenn wanted the house to look nice for her grandmother's visit. After running up the steps, he entered his son's rooms and kissed each one.

All breathing. All safe in their beds.

He could hear Grandma Helen's light snoring and kept going toward the master bedroom to see if Jenn was okay. He gave her a small shake before gently kissing her forehead.

"I love you," he whispered.

"I love you, too," she mumbled, and her eyes flew open. "Bob, why are you here?" She hugged him, then said, "I thought you had a meeting in the morning."

"Got fortunate, caught an early flight home." His lips lingered on her forehead.

"But—" Jenn was tired, slurring her words. She always did that when she was tired.

"Go back to sleep," he told her. "I'm going to decompress in front of the television downstairs. I'm a little wound up."

Relief flooded his heart as he pulled off the heavy suit and dropped it onto a chair. Maybe he had only imagined the voice.

He padded downstairs in his bare feet. "Okay," he said to the empty family room "I'm home. You happy?" No one answered, but that was okay. He was glad to be home.

JENN

Bob kissed me awake at 12:15 a.m.

At 1:15 a.m., something woke me up.

"Bob!" I called from the top of the steps, "I smell smoke." I hesitated when he didn't answer. Had he fallen asleep down there? "Bob, wake up. I think maybe a palm tree has been hit by lightning."

Remembering Grandma had arrived earlier that night, I went into the guest room and woke her up, too. "Grandma Helen, get up. We need to check the house."

"Jennifer? What's going on?" Her voice trembled. "What is it?"

"Probably nothing, but I smell smoke."

I went downstairs and saw Bob at the back door. He was looking out at the yard. "The palm trees in the backyard are intact. I'll check out front."

At that moment, I looked up and saw black smoke billowing out the vents of the vaulted ceiling.

"Bob, the house is on fire!" Horror chilled my blood as plumes of coal-black smoke crawled across the ceiling. I sent up a frantic prayer and ran toward the kids' rooms.

"Jenn," Bob yelled, "we have to save our babies!" Bounding up the steps two at a time, he scooped up the baby and our middle son, then lowered his head and charged down the stairs like the offensive tackle he used to be.

"Hurry," he cried. "I don't think we have much time."

Danny, our oldest son, has always been a heavy sleeper, so I grabbed him from the bed, cradling him to my chest. When he started to flail, I ordered him to hang on tight. "Danny, the house is on fire." His large brown eyes widened, so I clung tighter to him. "Remember when we practiced what to do if a fire started? This is it, and we have to get out." With Danny's arms around my neck, I ran toward the staircase.

"Stop, drop, and roll?" he mumbled sleepily. I lowered my head and ran toward the staircase. When I put him down, I reminded him, "Stay down, this is not a drill."

"Jennie, hurry!" Bob's baritone voice rang with the tension that thumped in my own ears. I handed Danny to Bob. I could hear Nathan and Gregory screaming downstairs, but I had to go back for my grandmother, who was just diagnosed with congenital heart disease and diabetes. We were warned she should not be overexcited.

Well, that ship had sailed.

I ran toward the guest room because she hadn't come out. Was she okay?

"Grandma, smoke is coming from the vents! We have to go!"

"I need my purse." She spoke in a high, thin voice. "I can't leave without my purse!"

Are you kidding me? She was taking her time, so I screamed, "The roof is on fire! Leave the purse."

Grandma ignored me. She slipped back into her room, snatched her purse off the dresser, and tightened her robe.

"Jenn, now!" Bob was seriously frantic. "*Now!*"

What was Grandma *doing*? The smoke thickened and lowered, becoming a dark blanket above the hallway ceiling. I dropped to my knees.

"Grandma, *now!*"

"I'm coming," she said, a thread of irritation in her voice. "I'm coming, but, I am *not* crawling on the floor."

"Then bend at your waist and lower your head. Move Grandma, move!"

"Wait, I can't go outside without my shoes."

"The house is on fire, Grandma. We could die!"

"I'm not leaving without my shoes!"

"Seriously? Just go, go, go, go!" My patience disappeared. I grabbed her arm and put her hand on the railing. Then, because she refused to budge, I reached into her room and grabbed her flats, which were next to the closet. Dark, blinding smoke stung my eyes and burned my lungs. I slammed the door, coughing, with her shoes in my hand.

What an idiot I'd been! I told my kids to never go back for anything, yet what did I do? I went back for a pair of $20 shoes.

Because the smoke was thickest in the guest room, and the guest room led to the attic, we knew the fire was directly over our heads, with only a thin sheet of drywall between us and the inferno. My lungs and eyes burned. My arms and legs trembled, and I don't remember descending the stairs, but when we reached the first floor, the front door wouldn't open. The latch on the door was always finicky, requiring a push and a pull at just the right angle.

As we all stood in the entryway with smoke filling the open space, I told the boys to get on the floor. Gregory, the baby, was in my arms clutching a blanket, so I pulled it over his face. My other sons clung to my legs.

"Stand back!" Bob bellowed. Then he used all his strength to yank the door open. The latch broke and Grandma called, "Good thing Bob is here. He is a beast."

The dense smoke followed us out of the house and surrounded us as we stood on the front porch.

"We can't go out in that storm, we'll be electrocuted." Grandma wasn't wrong; lightning flashed in every direction, accompanied by torrential rain.

"Grandma, we need you to be brave." Bob's voice was patient. "Going out in the storm is safer than waiting in a burning house. Let's go, Jenn." With Danny on my hip, I reached out to steady Grandma.

"Don't treat me like an old woman, Jennifer Lynne." She pulled away. "Get your babies to safety. I'll be right behind you."

Bob lowered his head like a linebacker and ran, his bare feet splashing on the pavement as he carried our toddler and three-year-old son in his muscular arms. I considered going through the side yard, but it was full of Jumping Cholla cactus, which made that route a bad idea, especially in bare feet.

Sheets of rain pelted our backs as we ran to the safety of our neighbor's front porch. Thunder shook the ground, and a lightning bolt lit the neighborhood. As Bob pounded on the neighbor's door, he pulled his soaked family into a sheltered corner and protected us with his body.

Tom Collins, a retired detective, peered out the window and answered Bob's frantic knocking in his underwear.

"What—Bob? Jennie? What happened?" Clearly, we'd awakened him.

"Fire." Bob's baritone was calm, but loud enough to be heard over the thunder. "Hit by lightning." My breathless husband pulled us into the tile foyer of their house.

"Come in, um—I need to get some clothes on." Tom ran to his bedroom and yelled to his wife. "Nancy, the Porters' house is on fire!"

Peeking out for a second, Nancy assessed the situation and appeared with a stack of towels in her arms. Trust the mother of four sons to be prepared in an emergency.

"Jenn, call 911!" Bob said, helping Grandma Helen to a chair. I nodded and ran toward the kitchen, looking for a phone. Tears from my stinging eyes ran down my face, and I wiped them with the back of my hand.

"What is the nature of your emergency?" The 911 operator sounded efficient but bored.

Breathless, I tried to explain. "Our house is on fire, I think it was struck by lightning."

"What is your exact location?"

My mind went blank. Clutching the phone in trembling fingers, I stood in my neighbor's kitchen and stared at my bare feet. "I—I don't know."

My gaze lifted to the vaulted ceiling as I searched for an answer. I couldn't remember my own address! The cool cleanliness of their kitchen struck me as I searched for some clue.

How could anyone forget where she lived? *Please God, help me remember, what is my address?*

My childhood address came to my lips, and I shook my head. I pushed my dripping hair out of my eyes and shivered as eight addresses in the past eight years came to mind. This was the first home we had ever owned, and it was probably going to burn to the ground.

I finally stuttered out, "I don't remember."

The operator sighed. "I can't send the firetruck without an address." Tears of frustration added to the burning sensation in my eyes.

"Bob," I was crying by that point, "what is our address?" Bewilderment and exhaustion filled my voice. My mind was completely blank. Where were we? Delaware? No, we moved to Arizona. Bob was offered a job as vice president if he was willing to move. I could picture the blueprints for our house; it had all the

CHAPTER FOURTEEN: GO HOME?

features I always admired. We chose the floor plan, colors, and fixtures. The house was in a perfect location. Scottsdale address, Paradise Valley Schools, Phoenix utilities, and Danny was accepted into Scottsdale Christian Academy and would be starting first grade in September.

The address? It wasn't as if we had just moved; we watched the construction progress, day after day. I knew every aspect of that house, but the address eluded me. My fingers seized with a cramp. As if my hand belonged to someone else, I watched the fingers tremble, like a person with Parkinson's. My chest hurt, and I felt sick.

I don't know how long I stood there dripping on Nancy's pristine floor, but Tom gently pried the phone from my hand. "Hello," he told the operator. "Yes, the address is—"

"5144 East Aire—" his wife yelled from the other room.

"I've got it, Nancy." He turned to the wall. "5144 East Aire Libre Avenue, corner of 52nd Street and East Aire Libre, two-story house, yes, at the dead end. Uh-huh, Tom Collins. No, the house belongs to Robert and Jennifer Porter." He hung up, then breathed deeply and announced that the firemen were on their way.

Bob stood at the window, waiting. Although it took the fire department about only five minutes to arrive, the passing time felt like hours.

"Who forgets their own address?" Tom patted my hand while I moaned.

"Jennie, people forget their own names after trauma. It's normal."

I could smell smoke in my wet hair and gratefully accepted another towel from Nancy. The first towel was covered with black soot. I was glad we had become friends with Nancy and Tom while we were building the house. In their eyes now, I saw understanding and compassion.

Nancy patted my arm. "It'll be okay, you'll see."

She gave me a cup of hot tea, which sloshed over the edge of the cup onto my soaked pajama bottoms. Why couldn't I steady my hands? I was shaking uncontrollably, and my body began to ache. I felt stiff, as if the rush of adrenaline had left me utterly depleted.

Outside, a symphony of sirens from police, an ambulance, and firetrucks filled the air. The emergency wails were answered by booming thunder and rhythmic sheets of rain that slammed against the house. The storm was still with us. Those poor firefighters!

I looked up, saw my neighbors' smoke alarm, and I realized I had never heard an alarm at our house. "Our fire alarms didn't go off. I don't remember hearing the smoke detectors, either." I kissed Gregory's warm head. "Bob, did the smoke detectors and fire alarms go off?"

He didn't answer but kept staring out the window facing our driveway.

"Grandma, did *you* hear the smoke alarm?"

"No," she answered from the family room. "No, dear, I heard no smoke alarms."

"The smoke detectors and fire alarms are all brand new." My temper flared. "What good is a detector that doesn't detect?"

Nancy looked at me quizzically, "Jennie, if you didn't hear anything, how did you know to get out?"

I looked at the high ceiling and frowned. "I'm not sure." I bit my lip, thinking. "Bob came in at 12:15 a.m. and kissed me awake." She stared as if urging me to get to the point, so I continued. "I asked him why he was home."

I turned to my husband. "Honey, what made you come home tonight? Grandma Helen came to help me with the kids."

"Maybe," he said slowly, "I just wanted to sleep in my own bed."

I frowned. That explanation didn't make sense.

Bob's voice hardened. "Maybe I don't need a reason, I just wanted to be with you and the kids. I got the last flight out before the storm."

To his credit, he always tried to get home if he could, and I nodded before continuing, my voice as shaky as my hands. "So, Bob kissed me awake, and I thought I was dreaming because I remembered he had meetings the next day."

Bob picked up the story. "I told Jenn to go back to sleep and decided to decompress in front of the television downstairs."

Nancy nodded. "But how did you know to get your family out?"

"It was the strangest thing . . ." I stopped. "I feel like I flew out of bed and landed on my feet. I remember telling the Lord I wasn't afraid of thunderstorms, so why was I shaking? My head itched, my scalp felt alive, like when the kids brought home lice from preschool. My hair was standing on end. Oh . . ." I lifted a brow as understanding dawned. "I must have been close to the lightning strike."

Nancy scratched her head. "I hate lice!"

Bob smacked his forehead. "You had to be close to the strike; that is why you're shaking so bad. And why flames are shooting out the roof over our bedroom."

I held up my hand—it was still quivering.

Tom considered, then looked at me. "You were sleeping on a waterbed, right?"

I nodded.

"Jenn, it's a miracle you aren't dead. No wonder you're shaking!"

I rubbed the towel over my wet head and continued. "I didn't know why I was shaking so hard, but the lightning—that does make sense."

When the firetrucks arrived, Bob and Tom went to the front door to watch the firefighters unload the hoses.

I drew Nancy aside. "When I woke up and was praying, I realized I was bleeding, really bleeding. I'd just finished my period less than a week before, so it didn't make sense. I also had a metallic taste in my mouth, like I'd bitten my tongue. That taste is still there."

Another slam of thunder shook the house.

"Mommy!" Gregory screamed as several bursts shook the house. Tears rolled down our toddler's face as I crooned, "One, one thousand, two, one thousand . . ."

Gregory held on tight and hid his face under the towel before shoving his two middle fingers into his mouth. "That means—"

"The storm is close," Nathan said.

Lightning flashed again, and Danny, not to be outdone, said, "God's fireworks."

Pulses of lightning sent jagged light into the kitchen. My oldest son looked at me accusingly. "You said we were safe inside the house. You promised the lightning wouldn't get us in the house."

Lifting my hands, I shrugged. "I'm sorry, honey, I didn't know it could." Danny seemed satisfied by my honesty, but the frown remained on his face.

He trusted me to know these things.

One of the firemen approached Bob and Tom.

"Hey, whose house is this?"

"Mine," Bob answered. "Can you save it?" Flames were shooting from the northeast corner of the roof over the master bedroom.

"Honestly—" the firefighter shook his head, "these houses are stick construction, and once they light up, there's not much hope." Bob stood watching the flames and prayed, asking God to save our house.

They were able to save our six-month-old home, although the structure suffered approximately $85,000 in damages. The lightning ran behind the wall in the kitchen and bedroom, shot into the attic, and blew a ten-foot hole in the roof. That jolt also tossed me out of bed. We were told a fireball shot through the attic, causing the entire space to burst into flame.

One of the inspectors asked Bob, "Where were you when the lightning struck?"

Bob told him he'd gone downstairs to watch TV.

"Good thing," the man replied. "If you'd been in that bed, you would've most certainly been killed."

Not only was it a miracle for "everything to fall into place" for Bob to make it home and get us all out of the house safely, but another miracle occurred. Something happened—I'm not sure what—but my Lyme disease disappeared that night. I was healed in the flash that blew me out of bed.

Years after these events, Bob gave me details I never heard before—how he heard the voice in the back seat and how he had to sprint through the airport to catch that last flight. He didn't see an angel or white feathers or a glowing orb. He did, however, feel the hands that lifted him to safety when he fell down some concrete steps, and the night of the fire, he heard a simple message that sent him home.

I can't imagine how we would have survived the fire without Bob.

"Go home?" He smiled when he shared the story with me. "I didn't have to be told twice."

Jennifer Porter earned a bachelor of science degree in education from Ashland University. After the fire, Jenn and Bob found a place to worship, and she began writing choral skits and dramas for Chaparral Christian Church in Scottsdale. After nearly nine years in Arizona, the Porters moved to Ohio to be closer to family and are now empty-nesters. They have been married for thirty-six years and are enjoying the delight of being grandparents.

ANGEL GLIMPSES

Criteria for Discerning an Angel Encounter

We can expect a true angel encounter to have at least these characteristics:

- The angel will seem to be an ordinary man or a recognizably supernatural being.
- The angel will deliver a message from God, call us to a special mission, or rescue us from an imminent danger.
- The angelic messenger might tell us something about our future—and if it is a true encounter, the prediction always comes true.
- Our initial reaction to an angel encounter may well be one of astonishment and fear.
- An angel encounter will not cause us to focus our thoughts on angels but to deepen our faith and commitment to the Lord—the One Who sent the angels.
- A true angel encounter will also lead us to greater obedience to the Lord and His Word.[23]

CHAPTER FIFTEEN

TENNIS SHOE ANGEL

YVONNE VOLLERT-NOBLITT WITH CAYLEN D. SMITH

The days before Christmas were hectic, especially for a mother of two. All the shopping centers were crowded with people buzzing here and there.

My first child was on a playdate at her friend's house, so I thought it would be a good time to stock up on some groceries. I took my youngest, Brett. He was almost one, old enough to not be too much of a handful as we walked down the long aisles stocked with food.

Once I had all the items on my grocery list, I went to my usual cashier. She was a sweet girl and we had become friends over the years. We said our hellos and she commented on how adorable Brett looked. He wasn't focused on her, though, but kept looking at something under the grocery cart. She laughed off his inattention and asked me about my day. I asked what she was planning for the holiday. With so many different events during the season, most people scrambled to visit families in other parts of the country.

She finished scanning my items and began to bag my groceries. I was trying to fish my checkbook from my handbag while making sure Brett remained upright in the shopping cart.

That's when I felt that premonition of disaster. Maybe it was sparked by the touch of Brett's shirt as it swept over my fingertips. My world unraveled in that instant.

One second Brett was sitting in the cart, then he was gone.

I don't know how he slipped out of my grasp, but he went headfirst over the side of the cart and was lying on the concrete floor, silent and still.

Strange what the body does when a rush of panic sweeps through your chest. I wanted to scream, but I had to listen for Brett. Why wasn't he crying? He was motionless, soundless, like a child's toy doll. I scooped him off the floor. His body was limp in my arms, utterly lifeless.

A thousand thoughts flitted through my mind. Was he dead? Brain damaged? Had he broken his spine or fractured his skull? Had I already heard his last cry?

All I wanted was to see him flinch, but he didn't.

I looked at the cashier, who appeared as shocked and helpless as I felt. As I stood there, too horrified to speak or pray or cry out, I heard squeaking noises. As I stared down at my pale boy, a pair of white tennis shoes appeared in my field of vision.

I looked up. A young man stood beside me, an average man and the only person in the store who had the presence of mind to help me.

His calm sent a wave of comfort washing over me. "Can I pray for you?" he asked. His question was simple, yet I seized on it as though it were a lifeline. "Yes!"

We bowed our heads over my son. The young stranger rested one hand on my shoulder and the other on top of Brett's head. As his words flowed, I immediately felt peace.

He prayed for Brett's recovery and for my anxiety, asking God to be present for me. Then he concluded his prayer with, "In Jesus's name, Amen."

I opened my eyes and again saw those white tennis shoes. Then I heard the sweet sound of a baby's cry. Brett's crying. He was awake.

Joy filled my heart, and I glanced up, wanting to thank the stranger, but the man in the tennis shoes had disappeared.

Holding tightly to my crying son, I turned to the cashier. Her eyes were wide, her mouth slightly agape, but I had to ask. "Y—you saw him, didn't you? Where did he go?" I lifted myself on tiptoes to look over the magazines and checkout stand, but I couldn't see him.

The cashier shook her head. "I don't know—he just disappeared." She looked toward the exits to see if she could spot the man walking out of the store. She turned back to me with a defeated shrug.

How could this guy have vanished? Had he run off, someone could have spotted him for me—identified him so I could catch up and thank him properly.

But no one pointed him out, and no one near us wore white tennis shoes.

I gently shushed my son and comforted him in my arms.

Then it hit me: I had met an angel. This encounter could not have taken place in my imagination. Besides, I had a witness—the cashier.

Just to make sure, I put Brett back in the cart and pushed it out into the parking lot, but the man in the white tennis shoes was nowhere around.

He had to have been an angel.

Years later, Brett and I were traveling in the mountains. The road became glutted with ice and snow, impossible for us to make any headway.

We were stuck.

Then a car came passing through, and a man stopped to see if we were okay. When we told him our tires couldn't make it through the ice and snow, without hesitation he helped us put chains on our tires.

Brett mentioned the man who helped us must have been another angel. Maybe it was the same angel who helped him in the grocery store.

So you see, I have always told my children about angels. About how the Lord sends them to protect and watch over us.

Brett went to Oregon for college and obtained a degree. Never once did he suffer from falling out of the grocery cart that day. God was merciful to us.

Often, when I went back to the grocery store, that cashier would greet me and say, "Remember that day when the man came to pray for you?" After all this time, she has not forgotten. She witnessed that encounter and is still affected by it.

That experience and many others serve to remind me angels are real and will keep watch over us. My family and I will always remember the young man who stepped out of thin air and disappeared the same way he came.

Our angel in tennis shoes.

Yvonne Noblitt lives in Southern California and continues to see God's amazing grace. She is the wife of Randy Noblitt and the mother of two adult children and stepmother of three. Professionally, Yvonne is a writer and producer of Christian media for radio and the web. **Caylen D. Smith** is a recent graduate of Azusa Pacific University and the author of five young-adult fantasy adventure novels. In her spare time, you can find her drawing, reading, or writing her next project.

ANGEL GLIMPSES

I do not know how to explain it; I cannot tell how it is,
but I believe angels have a great deal to do with the
business of this world.

—Charles H. Spurgeon[24]

CHAPTER SIXTEEN

THE ANGEL WORE BURBERRY

MARLENE RICE

I n 1967, during the middle of my senior year, I embarked on a spiritual journey. I had friends I spent time with on campus, but after school, I did very little with them because I never quite fit in.

I know feelings aren't facts. But I really didn't fit in with the cheerleaders, the athletes, the drama students, or the brainiacs. I knew them all, but I lived on the fringe of what was considered mainstream for high school students. Subsequently, my interior and exterior lives were equally boring.

That year, the Beatles rose to the top of the charts, and George Harrison was quoted as saying, "The Beatles saved the world from boredom." I found that to be only partially true. My passion for music transformed with every new group or singer to come along. Bob Dylan, Jefferson Airplane, Janice Joplin, Jimi

Hendrix, and the Rolling Stones only temporarily diminished my indifference to life.

I became a fan of musicians with transcendental qualities. Whereas my friends searched for meaning in "Sgt. Pepper's Lonely Hearts Club Band," I theorized imperfect truth was revealed in songs with lyrics birthed from psychedelic visions.

Trapped in a cycle of mediocrity, I saw no way of escape until I met Flynn Sanders, a chemistry student at one of the local universities. Flynn kept a key to the school lab. After hours, when everything was closed and locked up tight, he went back to the lab to mix chemicals. Before long, Flynn was making LSD available to the general public.

I was a seventeen-year-old high school student, yet Flynn found me reliable and trustworthy. He hired me to deliver his fresh-brewed compound to customers living in Los Angeles and the Orange County beach communities. Laguna Beach, Costa Mesa, and Newport Beach proved to be extremely profitable distribution points for his product. Flynn paid me well, and I was soon liberated from working the night shift at Jack in the Box.

Although many of my friends were dropping acid and claiming it heightened their spiritual awareness, I didn't experience the same effects. My drug-induced trips brimmed with unpleasant hallucinations and endless rounds of paranoia.

I met many interesting people through Flynn's impressive client list. Film producers and directors, actors, band members, professors, and even lawyers and judges were among his clients. But none proved to be more interesting than the individual I met on Woodland Drive in Laguna Canyon. The canyon is situated right before you enter idyllic, unspoiled Laguna Beach. Once a delightful, sleepy haven for local artists, Laguna Canyon became a thriving hippie colony.

I met Flynn at the lab, and he handed me a camouflage canvas backpack. When I asked who was receiving the product, he said,

"Don't worry, you'll know when you see him." Flynn reminded me no money was to change hands. This transaction was a gift.

Later, I walked up Woodland Drive and saw the cottage where I was to meet my contact. It was a small white clapboard structure with yellow trim and an indigo blue front door. Flower pots filled with seaside daisies, coastal sunflowers, and thick-stemmed jade plants framed the small wooden porch. I knocked on the door and patiently waited. An older man dressed in white linen with innumerable strands of beads draped around his neck greeted me with a welcoming hug and invited me inside.

I immediately recognized him; he was Timothy Leary, the famed controversial psychologist who advocated the use of LSD, especially to young people. He was the counter culture's psychedelic guru and popularized the phrase, "turn on, tune in, drop out." President Richard Nixon called him "the most dangerous man in America."

I emptied the contents of the backpack onto the center of a blue tablecloth adorning the kitchen table. Each vial was filled with LSD cut with purified distilled water. Leary immediately passed the vials to his disciples, who huddled around him like baby birds waiting to be fed.

A man with thick black dreadlocks insisted I stay for the festivities. Twenty people filled the small living room. In perfect unison, we followed Leary's lead and obediently sat on cushions on the floor. Folding our legs, we assumed the lotus position and began to meditate. Within ten minutes, my legs started to ache. No matter how much I wanted spiritual enlightenment, I could never attain it sitting in that position. I felt like a pretzel begging to be untangled.

A young man with curly blond hair appeared from out of nowhere. He knelt and whispered, "I think it's time for you to leave." I relished the thought and could hardly wait to get out of there. I rose, leaned into Timothy Leary, and conveyed my gratefulness for having had the opportunity to share airspace with him. He nodded and I made my exit. Before stepping outside, I stopped for a moment and looked around for the blond-haired guy, but he was nowhere in sight.

The next day I learned that drug enforcement agents raided Woodland Drive thirty minutes after I left. Many people were arrested. Had I stayed longer, I might have been one of those sitting in jail.

Relaxing in Hillcrest Park, I laid my bike down and found a sunny spot to sit. My thoughts drifted back to Laguna Canyon and how I narrowly escaped a drug bust. Could someone be watching over me? An invisible force that saw beyond my faults? A presence greater than myself who believed I was worthy of redemption?"

I found my tribe amid the hippie movement. But situations such as what I experienced on Woodland Drive left me feeling spiritually empty and unfulfilled. Only for brief moments did I feel anything remotely sacred. I had a God awareness. But I couldn't define Who or What He was.

The inevitable finally occurred—Flynn Sanders made a mistake. He was working in the school lab when something—no one knows what—caused an explosion.

Fire engines quickly arrived at the scene. With lights flashing and sirens sounding, an ambulance appeared and took Flynn to the hospital. The incident was in all the local newspapers the next morning. Flynn was badly burned and spent months recovering in the hospital. The police didn't take long to discover what he had been doing. Flynn was expelled from the university, and I lost touch with him.

My sweet, kindhearted parents were understandably distraught over the direction my life was going. In January of my senior year, I turned eighteen, and the day after my birthday I moved out. I rented a small studio apartment and hung an iridescent peace sign in the front window. Somehow, I managed to stay in school and graduated with my senior class. The ceremony came to an end, I hopped in a friend's car, and we headed to the Monterey Pop Festival. My self-centered attitude and narcissistic behavior blinded me from seeing the pain I was causing my parents.

My future was not going as planned, and I continued to cause my parents more misery. One afternoon, I told Mom I wanted to meet with her. She panicked because my dad was unable to join us. Not wanting to be alone with me, Mom invited Betty, a family friend, to join us. I agreed Betty would be a good buffer.

I wasn't sure how mom was going to take the news I was moving to a hippie commune in Southern Oregon. I felt confident that, even if Betty didn't agree the move to a hippie commune was in my best interest, she understood I was a free spirit and given to spontaneity.

As the words *move* and *hippie commune* rolled off my tongue, Mom collapsed in Betty's arms. Betty was a nurse and told me where to find the smelling salts in Mom's medicine cabinet. Dad rushed home and did his best to reassure Mom I was the most stable of my entire group of friends. He was confident that one day I would wake up and live a normal, productive life. I don't know if Dad's words helped console my mom. It took years for her to forgive me for the poor decisions I made in the sixties.

Most people in the commune wanted to live a self-sufficient, off-the-grid life. My friends and I were not nearly as hard-working; our focus was on spiritual matters. We incorporated yoga and meditation into a daily routine. Everyone spent hours sitting in a full lotus position outside under the pine trees. However, I became restless after sitting for only ten minutes. Finally, I resolved I had too much energy. Early morning yoga was worse than having ten root canals without Novocaine.

I considered giving up my spiritual odyssey, but then I ran into a guy who was walking down Takilma Road. I was looking up at a hawk circling above when I collided with this poor unsuspecting fellow. The large leather book he was carrying flew out of his hands and spiraled downward. Lunging forward, I caught the book before it hit the ground.

Apologizing for the mishap, I asked him to forgive my negligence in watching where I was going. He smiled. "No problem."

Before handing the book over, I peered at the title and recognized the words. I saw them on a book at my Grandma Ceretti's house: *Holy Bible*. I handed him his book and continued walking.

Later that day, I stopped by Diane's house. I found her in the kitchen making vegetable soup on the wood-burning cookstove. Glancing at the dining table, I saw the same black leather book I had seen earlier. I asked Diane where the book came from, and she responded, "I have no idea. You know how many people come through here. Someone must have left it." She promptly picked up the book and handed it to me, saying, "Take this, no one here is interested in reading it."

I took the Bible and made my way down to the river. Spying a large flat rock, I sat down and began to read. I started in Genesis, then jumped ahead to Psalms and Proverbs. The more I read, the more I believed the book had something for me. I turned to the New Testament and devoured the first four gospels.

In one month, I read that entire Bible. A beautiful illustration of an angel adorned one of the pages, and I discovered a section in the back called a concordance. I looked up words in the concordance, and it directed me to Bible verses containing that word. I was surprised to discover the word *angel* appeared 296 times in the Old and New Testaments.

Angels fascinated me. I read every verse that pertained to angels. I was amazed by the important role they play in God's divine plan. I came to believe it didn't matter if I ever saw an angel myself; I was confident their presence would be made known to me if it was necessary.

A few days later, James, an old friend, appeared on my doorstep. James was a notorious marijuana smuggler, moving pot from

Mexico up the west coast and into Canada. I immediately noticed a change in him since the last time we had met. His long, braided ponytail was missing and so was his heavy, dark beard. But the difference was more than a physical change. An honest gentleness and warmth emanated from him. This was not the same greedy, egocentric drug dealer I once knew.

I invited James in and asked what he had been doing since we last saw each other. "I've been singing in the choir at my church in Anaheim, California," he said, smiling.

I was taken aback by his answer and encouraged him to share the story of his transformation. We stayed up all night talking about Jesus. I had so many questions, and James patiently answered all of them. At the end of his visit, he prayed with me. I entered a new awareness and confidently believed Jesus was the missing piece of the puzzle of my life.

The spiritual enlightenment I sought had been in front of me all along. As a teenager, friends took me to church youth groups and Christian summer camp. I learned God existed when my dad's business partner's wife and their kids picked me up for Vacation Bible School. My Grandma Ceretti sent me colorful, illustrated Bible story books. My favorite teacher, Miss Benefeld, prayed with students when they were upset.

How did I miss the truth? Something so readily available and yet so elusive. I speculated I missed out on Jesus because I was determined to live my way, not God's way.

After careful thought and consideration, I got on my knees and prayed a simple prayer: "God, if you are real, I want you. If Jesus came to give me a new and abundant life, I want this life. Please forgive me and come into my heart. Amen!"

At that moment, my mind was permanently altered. Not because of drugs or Eastern thought or mysticism, Jesus revolutionized my thinking. God was present in my spirit, and my life profoundly changed. The Bible began to make sense, and the scriptures came to life as I read them.

Friends from church gave me books about modern people who encountered God and experienced miracles in their lives. One such book was *God's Smuggler*, the true story about Brother Andrew, a Dutch Christian. During the communist era, Andrew smuggled Bibles into countries where it was illegal for Christians to have even a page of the Word of God. Andrew and his organization, Open Doors, still take Bibles and other faith-building materials to Christians in countries where faith costs the most.

The book *God's Smuggler* changed my life. It was exciting to read about divine encounters and angelic visitations making it possible for Open Doors' team members to deliver their precious cargo to believers living under persecution.

Little did I know that fifteen years later I would be working for Andrew at his U.S. office. When I joined Open Doors, one of my responsibilities was to organize Bible-smuggling trips from the United States into China, Cuba, Vietnam, the Soviet Union, and Eastern Europe.

In the early 1980s, I took my first Bible-smuggling trip into mainland China. Eighteen of us were on the team: Australians, Hong Kong Chinese, Americans, and one Canadian. We covertly carried two thousand Chinese Bibles from Hong Kong to Beijing. The Bibles were then dispatched to Christians living in remote parts of China.

The individual suitcases for which we were each responsible were prepacked in Hong Kong with Chinese Bibles. We didn't see or handle the suitcases until we got off the plane in Beijing and went to baggage claim. All I knew was I had to collect three suitcases. My bags would be identifiable by the purple ribbon tied to the handles.

The plan seemed simple enough. I was to watch for the three marked suitcases to come around on the conveyor belt. I was to grab them, put them onto an airport luggage cart, and roll them through security praying I would not be asked to put them through the X-ray machine. I was then to push the cart outside, where two vans and four Chinese nationals waited to load the suitcases. The cargo was to be driven and delivered to Christians who were anxiously awaiting their first Bibles.

I did not foresee any problems; in fact, I felt quite capable of accomplishing my task. Unfortunately, I encountered a crisis of monumental proportion.

The most important thing on a Bible-smuggling trip is to blend in. My only experience of anything Chinese was eating in the Chinese restaurant on Balboa Island a few miles from where my husband and I lived with our four children. Everything in that restaurant was red.

The trip took place in December, so Beijing would be cold. Wanting to make sure I blended in with everything Chinese, I purchased a bright red bomber jacket.

After safely landing at the Beijing Airport, I stepped off the plane and noticed I was the only one in the airport wearing red. I later learned Mao favored somber colors, so the people wore olive green, gray, and navy Mao jackets. No one wore red.

I made my way to baggage claim and discovered every luggage cart had been seized by passengers who exited the plane ahead of me. My confidence began to diminish.

We were on a serious mission. Once in baggage claim, team members were not to talk to each other. If the guards suspected you of bringing anything illegal into China, you did not want to bring your teammates down with you. If you were apprehended, no one from the group could help you. The guards would confiscate your bags and might hold you overnight for questioning.

Armed guards cruised throughout the baggage claim area, their eyes raking over each of us. I made my way to the conveyor belt and watched for the suitcases with purple ribbons. I noticed Jess, a team member from Australia, struggling with a suitcase. The weight of the bag was apparently more than she expected.

I turned back to the conveyor belt. I could see my first bag coming toward me, the purple ribbon secured to the handle. I felt adrenaline pump through my body. All I needed to do was lift the suitcase off the conveyor belt and place it on the floor. I kept telling myself, "You can do this."

My suitcase turned the corner and was almost within reach. I leaned over and grabbed the handle. Then the unthinkable happened. The bag was so heavy I couldn't lift it. A loose strap caught my hand and pulled me onto the carousel. The next thing I knew, I was lying on top of the suitcase, circling baggage claim.

I passed two of the Hong Kong team members. Their eyes widened with horror. Three of the Americans looked on and tried not to laugh. Out of the corner of my eye, I saw a group of airport guards gazing at me in disbelief.

Suddenly, two guards ran over to help me. Working in tandem, they lifted me off the conveyor belt and set me on the floor. When I was out of harm's way, one of the guards gripped the handle of my suitcase and scarcely got it off the carousel. The look on his face paralyzed me. I could tell he was already wondering what I could have put in my suitcase that weighed so much. And who packs a suitcase they can't even lift?

My instincts told me to remain calm. I would get through this. I ran over to my suitcase and bowed to the two guards. I was so flustered I forgot how to say *thank you* in Chinese and said "Gracias" instead. They laughed and replied, "Gracias," but with a Chinese accent. Then one of them inquired, "Spanish?" and I said "Si." A Chinese woman began to translate for me, and I found out that one of the guards had a niece studying in Barcelona.

Thinking I was Spanish, the guard was happy to meet someone from the country hosting his niece. I kept bowing and repeating, "Si, si." They turned and marched back to the X-ray machines. I felt relieved, but I wasn't home free yet. There were still two more bags for me to retrieve. With no luggage carts in sight, I pulled my first suitcase over to a pillar and pushed it out of sight.

Returning to the conveyor belt, I planted my feet firmly on the floor. Another large bag with a purple ribbon came toward me. I braced myself and dragged the bag off the carousel and pushed it behind the pillar next to the first bag. One more bag to go. This time with careful precision, I positioned myself to pull the bag up and set it on its side. It was an awkward maneuver but required less strength than lowering the suitcase to the floor.

Finally, all three of my suitcases were hidden behind the pillar.

Now I faced an even bigger dilemma. By that time, my teammates had made it safely through security. I was the only foreigner among a sea of Chinese faces, and I could not find a cart to help me get my bags through customs.

Struggling to hold back tears, I prayed: "Dear God, please send help. I cannot do this by myself. If I ever needed a guardian angel to show up, Lord, now would be the time. Amen!" Instantly, I felt a peace come over me. I stood and turned around.

There he was, only ten feet away. A tall, mysterious man appeared from out of nowhere. His skin had a warm bronze glow and he was wearing a handsome, charcoal-colored cashmere coat. The noise in the baggage claim area hushed. I felt as though he and I were the only ones in the room.

With careful attention, he raised his right hand and pointed toward a heavy black curtain and motioned for me to go there. I walked past several guards who appeared oblivious to my presence and went directly to the curtain. I looked over my shoulder and saw the man nod in another direction. I followed his lead and there it stood. Behind the curtain was one lone luggage cart. With amazed pleasure, I rolled the cart over to my bags and loaded all three.

I turned to say thank you to the man in the cashmere coat, but he was gone, nowhere to be seen. Later, when I thought more about it, I realized he was standing alone, without any luggage of his own. Odd.

I got to customs with my three suitcases filled, and the guard at the X-ray machine didn't even look up. He just lifted his hand and waved me through. All my team members were outside waiting. The Australians helped load the remaining bags into the van, and we waved to our courageous Chinese brothers as they drove off to deliver their sacred cargo.

Everyone loaded their personal items into taxis and headed over to the hotel. I told the team I had something to do and would catch up with them.

I stepped back into the now-deserted baggage claim area and walked over to the spot the mysterious man had occupied. Could he have been an angel sent to help me escape the watchful eyes of armed guards?

I saw no trace of his presence, then something caught my eye. I looked down; resting at my feet was a feather. I knelt and picked it up. Was this a feather from an angel's wing? No, it looked like a sparrow's tail feather, probably carried in on the sole of someone's shoe. Or maybe it drifted inside on a breeze.

But it really doesn't matter. I believe God strategically placed that feather in the place where the mysterious stranger stood as a reminder that angels will show up when I expect them least. And I can trust God to send angels when I—when *we*—need them most.

Marlene Rice was born in Canada but raised in Orange County, California. She's been married to Frank Rice for thirty-nine years, and they have four children, nine grandchildren, and one great-grandson. Marlene has worked and ministered in China, Cuba, Eastern Europe, Vietnam, Siberia, India, Jamaica, and Haiti. Her favorite things are people and life.

ANGEL GLIMPSES

In Old Testament terminology, angels are *sons of God* while men are *servants of God*. In the New Testament this is reversed. Angels are servants, and Christians are sons of God. This peculiar order may be due to the fact that, in the Old Testament, men are seen as related to this sphere over which angels are superior; while in the New Testament, saints are seen as related to their final exaltation into the likeness of Christ, compared to which estate the angels are inferior.[25]

CHAPTER SEVENTEEN

ANGELS SAVED FAITH

JUDY COMBS

I had long looked forward to this pack trip to snow camp. The trip wouldn't be an easy one—twelve miles, four hours on horseback, from the Glacier Peak Wilderness of the Washington Cascades to the four-thousand-foot-high Pacific Crest National Scenic Trail. The Trail runs 2,663 miles from Canada to Mexico, and it's as high as you can get and still be on a trail.

Frank, a fit sixty-five-year-old family friend, had packed with horses all his life; as a boy of fifteen, he learned from the old Colorado packers. My husband, Tom, encouraged me to learn from Frank. Frank's sweet wife Michi baked us cookies for the trail.

Frank rode General Lee, a big white Missouri Fox Trotter gelding, I was mounted on Rhema, a palomino Quarter Horse mare, and led my packhorse, Faith, a chestnut half-Arabian loaded with fifty-pound panniers (boxes) and a top pack. Both horses were raised and trained from birth on our five-acre farm in Duvall, Washington, nestled against the Cascade foothills.

We drove to the Milk Creek trailhead in our truck-horse trailer rigs. I eagerly anticipated learning how to camp in the snow with horses. With its forests and rushing creek, the Milk Creek Trail opened before us as we climbed the thirty-six switchbacks to the Pacific Crest Trail. There the view widened and leveled out at four thousand feet to expose the white summit of Glacier Peak. The only blown-down tree we came across was a small one, easily stepped over.

Only a remnant of the twelve-foot winter snowpack remained, enabling us to work into deepening snow to look for a place to camp. Firmly packed at this time of year, the snow muffled the soft thuds of the horses' hooves. They never floundered in the deep snow as we carefully searched for an appropriate spot. Faith decided she didn't like knee-deep snow and tried to leave. She got herself into a six-foot tree well, but Frank dallied her lead rope on his roping saddle and dragged her to a little swale against the side of the mountain. The melt exposed bare ground in that hollow, so we decided to make camp there. We had a 300-degree view of snow-draped mountains, and we did not have to stand on ice and snow. The drift from the slope above cupped around us and provided water for the horses to drink, so we tied them to scraggy dwarfed trees on the edge of the clearing.

Our packhorse would have made us the envy of any hiker because we were able to pack a propane heater and comfortable lawn chairs. Our spacious eight-by-ten-foot tent was furnished with a six-inch-thick king-sized air mattress with warm down sleeping bags that defied nature. I also had a hot water bottle to keep me comfy. While we ate a hot dinner of beef stew, our blanketed horses ate their evening meal of hay pellets and grain to warm them.

Comfortable and full, we relaxed in our chairs with a hot cup of cocoa and watched the sun go down, a molten display in a butterscotch sky. The moon rose, casting a bluish white light that painted our surroundings with a purplish hue.

The next morning, I looked out at the spectacular mountains and mused about the grandeur of God's creation. To my surprise, I thought I heard a sinister voice in my spirit say, *Ha, you can't do anything. You can't have anything. I can take it all from you in a moment, and you will have nothing.*

I gasped. Had I heard right? Where did that thought come from? I remembered the Bible story about how Satan sought permission from God to take everything from Job and God allowed it. But God rewarded Job for his faithfulness, and Job wound up with more than he had before.

As a believer of good conquering evil, I said, "In the name of Jesus, you have no power! You can do *nothing* without His permission. My life belongs to Jesus, and if I die and go to God, you still lose!" I bowed my head and submitted myself to the Lord, arming myself against the fear trying to upset me. "Lord God, I put my faith in You." Peace prevailed over my soul, but that peace would soon be tested.

By 11:00 a.m., we'd rolled up our tent and said goodbye to our mountain campsite where the peaks touched the sky. Leaving the Pacific Crest Trail behind, Frank and General Lee led the three of us down the Milk Creek trail cut out of the side of the mountain. As we dropped below the snowline, we came to the small tree blocking the trail. Faith had stepped over it on the way up, but now she refused it. She was usually a sweet and cooperative mare and as sure-footed as a mountain goat.

At first, we thought we understood her problem: She was either afraid to put her weight over the tree, or she was being stubborn. Animals have keen instincts and like to keep their feet on solid ground so they can flee if necessary. Horses learn on one side of their brains at a time, so an obstacle can look different to them on another occasion.

We dismounted to help her. Frank went to her head while I went to her rear to give support with a hand on her rump. Frank picked up her front foot to put it on the other side of the tree. She took her hoof out of his hands. He asked her again, giving her every chance to trust him, but she still refused.

By that time, we mistakenly thought she was being stubborn and decided to discipline her. I slapped her rear with my bare hand as Frank jerked her head with the lead. In the instant before I struck her, in my spirit I heard *No! Don't hit her!* God knew if we slapped her, we would only make matters worse.

As I hit her anyway, I retorted, *What do you mean, don't hit her!? She needs it!* I should have listened to that inner urging.

Faith panicked. Instead of going over the tree on the trail, she made the decision to step off the trail to go around it. This was a good, solid trail, but it wasn't wide enough for detours. Frank and I glanced at each other in total disbelief as Faith stepped onto the steep mountainside. I almost thought she'd make it, but to my horror, the dead weight of her load slammed against her, turning her so she faced empty air. Unable to keep herself on the side of the mountain, she slid and paddled, struggling to stay on her feet. She had to jump a log bigger than the one I was asking her to step over. A feeling of impending doom swept over as she plunged toward the trees below.

"Oh, no! God, help her! Do something!" The words came out of my mouth without conscious thought behind them. Then, as an afterthought, I added, "I know—send angels!"

Suddenly, I saw two ten-foot warriors hovering alongside the cliff in front of me. They were transparent but wore white robes I could see through. With calm authority, one of them asked me, "What do you want?"

"What do I want? Save my horse!"

On the mountainside, Faith was still scrambling to keep her balance as she fell.

"Do you want the load, too?" the angel asked.

Wasn't that a no-brainer? "Yes! Save her first, and the load second, okay?"

The first angel nodded at the second. "Let's go!" They zipped down the mountain faster than the speed of light, and I lost sight of them and my horse. I could still hear crashing sounds, though, but after a moment the mountain became ominously quiet.

Unaware of what I saw and heard, Frank blew out a breath. "Well, let's go down the mountain and see if you still have a horse."

We made a plan. Frank would work horizontally on foot to find Faith's tracks, while I rode down to the next switchback and worked upward as we shouted to each other for location. My mind was numb as I rode. Had I lost my horse?

Then I heard her whinny, asking me not to leave her, and I knew she was still alive. I hoped she was not so badly injured we'd have to put her down. If she had a broken leg, we'd have to shoot her or cut her jugular, and we hadn't brought a gun with us.

As I rode down, my mind filled with a song I had heard only once before. The words, which came from the Scriptures and spoke of mountains bowing down before the Lord, resonated in me. My mind kept repeating those words as I tried to wrap my mind around what had just happened.

When I reached the switchback, I tied Rhema to a tree and began to climb hand-over-hand through a tangle of logs. Driven by adrenaline, I didn't feel my fifty-five years. My slick cowboy boots slipped on a thousand years of wet pine needles as I clambered up through lofty pines growing horizontally out of the mountain before they arched upward.

After breaking onto the open slope, I paused and braced myself against a tree to gasp for air. Looking up, I saw my horse on a little bluff. She was standing above me, her ears pricked forward as she looked down at me.

I looked her over, realized she was fine, and called out to Frank as I mopped my brow. "I've got a horse! And she doesn't have any blood on her!!" The panniers were nowhere in sight, but the lawn chairs (of all things!) were still strapped to her back.

Apparently, the angels had scooped her up and carried her horizontally across the open ridge, between two trees almost too close together for a horse to fit through. She passed through, but the pannier boxes didn't and slammed against the trees. At that point, she must have jumped out of the harness and slid to the end of a little shelf where she stood and waited for us. Had she continued her downward trajectory, she would have fallen straight off a hidden cliff and broken her neck.

We later found the panniers intact, close to the trail below.

I climbed up onto the narrow shelf with her, finding barely enough room for both of us. I had to be careful lest she accidentally knock me off and hung onto her as I took the lawn chairs off her back—I didn't want them to get hung up as we took her down. There was no way she could have made it through the timber I had just climbed through, so I turned her around and tried to lead her. She pivoted on her back feet and stayed on the shelf, afraid to step toward the towering pines fifty feet away. If I could get her to the trees, we could work our way down to the trail by bracing from tree to tree, a distance of about 100 feet. I thought the ordeal was over and we would soon be on our way—but God was not finished yet.

As I tried to lead Faith, my foot slipped off the mountain. I barely managed to catch myself; then *I* was the one afraid to take another step. I hollered at Frank, "I can't move! I don't know what to do!"

He called back, "Get a stick and toe in footholds!"

I looked around, found a stick, and began to dig small holes where my foot could rest. I took four more cautious steps when I fell again, tried to catch myself, missed, and slid downward on my belly, desperately clawing to stop myself, looking for anything to hang onto. I grabbed a long root growing out of the mountain and hung on for dear life! The root was just long enough for me to grip with two hands, and somehow I still had ahold of Faith's twelve-foot lead.

I looked down at the tree below me, afraid I would slip and fall. Panic overtook me. "Oh, God!" I cried. "You didn't bring me this far to let me die now, did You?" My heart hammered in my chest as my hands slipped on the root. I was losing my grip and had nowhere to go but down.

My feet scrambled for purchase, sending scree bouncing down the mountain. My wrists were weakened by carpal tunnel, and my fingers slid to the last two inches of the root. In that last desperate second, with great deliberation, God spoke to me: *What would you do if you had faith?*

I didn't think this was a good time for discussion, but He had my attention. "If I had faith? Why, I'd let go!" I looked around, searching for anything I could grab. I noticed a big log embedded into the side of the mountain just beyond my reach. As a last-ditch effort, I could reach it if I swung on the root and launched myself in that direction. What did I have to lose?

I needed faith—and momentum.

I swung once, twice, and the third time I let go of the root, reached for the log, and caught it!

As I crawled upward toward safety, Frank called, "Come on now, you can't just stand there all day; you've got to do something!"

Panting, I said, "Can you see me?"

"Well, no," he drawled.

"Well, I've been kinda busy!"

Once I reached firm footing, I turned and surveyed the situation. In my leap to the log, I had dropped the lead, and I had to get it back. Faith was frozen. She wouldn't take a step unless she was asked to.

Frank, who had worked his way closer to me, said, "If you can reach that lead, toss it to me." I braced my feet on the log, stretched out on my belly, caught the lead, then tossed it over to him.

Faith knew we were trying to help her. Frank's hunting boots gave him just enough traction to bring her across one careful step at a time. As he brought her down, sliding from tree to tree, he beckoned for her to come to him each time he braced himself. That day, both Faith and I learned to obey with humility.

Safe again on the trail, Frank found our two fifty-pound panniers intact and within reach of the switchback. The angels stopped them where we could find them: fifty feet across from Faith and one hundred feet down. They could have slid past the end of those switchbacks and been lost forever, but they were right in front of us. They could not have moved fifty feet horizontally without divine intervention.

We lowered them with a rope, grateful we were able to rescue so much expensive camping gear.

Two and a half hours after our ordeal began, we had Faith loaded up again. Although we were exhausted and so thirsty we could have drunk the river dry, we were grateful to be in one piece. God had sent angels to rescue us. He rescued the horse first, then the load.

We didn't have to spend a dark night alone in the woods. Had we been injured, it would have taken twenty-four hours for help to arrive. We had no cell phones, and even if we had, it's nearly impossible to get a signal in the mountains.

Awed by the miracle we had received, we realized we still had a three-hour trip and thirty-five switchbacks ahead of us. We still had to ford the chest-deep waters of Milk Creek, scramble up the bank on the other side, and pick our way down the mountain over rocks and roots. Our legs braced against every downhill step that slammed us into the front of the saddle.

We arrived at our truck and horse trailer rigs about 5:30 p.m, six and a half hours after we left camp, two hours before nightfall. And we were not done. Before we could call it a day, we had to take care of our horses. They were as "played out" as we were.

We off-loaded three hundred pounds of packs, panniers, and saddles before we bedded, fed, and watered the horses. When they were settled, we got a well-deserved dinner ourselves and collapsed in our warm campers.

After breakfast the next morning, we drove out of the wilderness, then two hours south to Duvall, Washington.

My vet came out to check Faith. She was fine except for a slight harness burn on her chest and a fist-sized hematoma on her belly. The doctor said, "It's a miracle. Horses can get gouged just going through a gate, and all she got is a bruise."

Nevertheless, that experience made a better horse of Faith. She is now more cautious and willing to obey. I believe our adventure made a more obedient person out of me, too. If God says, "Jump," I say, "How high?" I stay on the trail of my faith and listen for the Word. It's a good trail, and I want to stay on it.

The next year Frank and I rode again in the same area. As we came down the backside of the loop on the Milk Creek Trail, Faith tugged a little as I coaxed her and clearly didn't want to go there. But I wanted to stop at the accident site to reminisce.

In spite of my protests, Frank climbed down after my lawn chair. Usually, a situation isn't as bad as remembered. Frank lowered himself, climbing down hand over hand until he got my chair and brought it back up! My souvenir is a little bent up, but I never see it without thinking *Praise the Lord!*

Judy Combs is an experienced mountain woman with more than twenty thousand miles horseback riding in the Cascade Mountains and the author of *God, Rocky Trails & the Mountains*. Her story will challenge your faith and stir you to know you are within the power of God's protection. She is the founder of Shiloh Prayer & Fasting Ranch, a faith-based ministry for the broken and wounded, as well as president of the John Wayne Wagons & Riders Club. At seventy-nine, she recently married missionary and pastor Dr. Bill Combs.

ANGEL GLIMPSES

> The angels are near to us. [They] have long arms, and,
> although they stand before the face and in the presence
> of God and His son Christ, they are hard by and about
> us in those affairs which by God we are commanded to
> take in hand.
>
> —Martin Luther[26]

CHAPTER EIGHTEEN

GUARDIANS AND MESSENGERS

BEVERLY FISH

We have all heard that guardian angels watch over us. In the summer of 1980, I was blessed to meet one of mine.

That day, my husband, Tim, and I were at Port Hueneme Beach with our toddler son, Ryan, and Tim's little sister Jenny, who was only twelve. Tim was relaxing on the beach, watching Ryan play in the sand, while Jenny and I were body-surfing in the waves.

Suddenly, I noticed I couldn't see Jenny anywhere, and I somehow had drifted way out, far past the breakers. I tried to swim in, but the current kept pulling me farther out. I remembered being told to swim parallel to the beach if you are caught in a riptide, but I was so exhausted from trying to fight the current all I could do was bob up and down, gasping for air.

I bobbed for what felt like a long time and realized no one could hear me scream, and the lifeguard was too far down the beach to see me floundering. Desperate, I cried out to God. I cried, "Lord, if this is my time to go, please take me quickly, but if it isn't my time, please send me help!"

I thrust my head up out of the water one last time to snatch a breath. That's when I saw a young, good-looking, blonde-haired man on a surfboard. He was coming right at me. Without saying a word, he lifted me onto the surfboard and paddled me into shore.

The entire time I was hanging onto that board, thanking him and telling him he'd just saved my life. He didn't answer, but when we reached the shallows, he helped me off the board, then took off toward the open water, paddling back to wherever he came from.

I stayed on the beach for a while, catching my breath and gathering my strength for the walk back to my family. When I finally made it back, Tim said, "Hi, babe, did you have a good time?"

I wanted to yell at him! But I composed myself and solemnly answered, "No, in fact, I got caught in a riptide and almost drowned. If it hadn't been for this surfer who came out of nowhere to save my life, I'd be gone!"

Tim blinked at me in surprise. "You mean a lifeguard, right?"

"No," I said, falling onto the towel beside him. "It was a nice young man. A surfer. He didn't have a flotation device or red shorts, it was just him and his surfboard."

Tim shook his head. "Babe, see that flag over there on the lifeguard station? That flag means there's no surfing allowed on this beach. Look, there are no surfers in the water or out of the water."

I looked, and Tim was right. No surfers anywhere, not even down the beach where I came ashore.

"Well—" I drew a deep breath. "All I know is I was rescued by a surfer after I prayed for God to help me." My eyes widened. "Wow, maybe it was an angel. Maybe that explains why he never said a word to me."

Tim lifted a brow, but he didn't argue.

While Jenny watched Ryan for us, Tim and I walked down the beach to see if we could find the surfer. As you can probably guess, there were no surfers anywhere—but there was one for me.

I was filled with thankfulness and awe to think God heard my cry and immediately sent a guardian angel to rescue me.

On another occasion, Tim and I went up the coast to Pismo Beach to spend the weekend at the Sea Crest Inn. That autumn weekend was beautiful, clear and warm. We went to our favorite seafood restaurant for lunch. While we were there, we both noticed this attractive, young black man sitting at the table next to ours. He was dressed casually, but I couldn't help noticing his boots—they were classic brown suede work boots, but they looked brand new.

When we finished our lunch, for some reason Tim and I felt drawn to go to him, say hello, and shake his hand. We didn't really talk to him, but just felt led to give him a friendly greeting. Then we left.

The next morning was Sunday, so we decided to walk down to the beach to spend time worshipping the Lord and praying together. As we walked along the paved path through the beautiful hotel grounds, we both hit a slick, wet, algae-covered spot on the sidewalk. Tim began to slip and so did I. Tim was able to catch his balance, but I fell and landed on my right ankle. Immediately, I felt excruciating pain, and although I tried to get up, I couldn't put weight on it. Tim helped me stand, and someone ran over with a lawn chair for me to sit in. While I sat there, sick and woozy from the pain, the person called 911 for us.

I was so embarrassed because I had thrown up all over myself and passed out from the pain. The paramedics didn't take long to arrive. They checked out my ankle and said they didn't think it was broken, but I would need an X-ray to be sure.

The first thing that popped into my mind was our big plans to go on a tour of Israel in three weeks. We were going with people from our church, and we were so looking forward to seeing the Holy Land for the first time. I hated to cancel because I'd done something as silly as mess up my ankle.

The paramedics asked if we wanted them to transport me to the nearest hospital, but because the injury wasn't life-threatening, Tim chose to drive me. After being carried to the car, I sat in the front seat feeling upset and depressed. Tim ran upstairs to pack our suitcases and check out since we had to head home soon.

As I sat there with the window open, the young man we had noticed the day before walked up, and I couldn't help noticing he was wearing the same outfit. Without so much as a hello, he said, "In ten days, you will be totally healed so you will be able to go on your trip."

Stunned, I thanked him, and he smiled. As he walked away, I saw he was wearing the same brand-new work boots he wore in the restaurant.

Was he a messenger angel?

When Tim came down with our bags, I told him what had happened. He went looking for the young man, but he couldn't find him anywhere.

We went to the emergency room at the hospital. After obtaining an X-ray, the doctor confirmed I hadn't broken any bones but suffered a severe sprain. I told him we were scheduled to go to Israel in three weeks and asked if my ankle would be healed enough to go.

He smiled and said my ankle would be back to normal in ten days.

I looked at him and thought how strange this doctor would say the same thing as that young man. But I believed them both.

We did not cancel our trip. I kept thanking God the swelling and pain were going to be gone by the tenth day, and guess what? They were! On the ninth day, my ankle was still swollen and painful, but on the tenth day, the swelling was gone and so was the pain!

God healed my ankle, and I'm convinced He sent a messenger angel to give me assurance so I would not cancel our trip. Tim and I went to Israel, walked all over the place, and I had no pain or swelling in my ankle at all. I felt as though I had never injured it. Thank you, Lord!

God is good—He knows what we need and when we need it, and sometimes He knows we need a little assurance.

Beverly Fish lives in Camarillo, California, with her husband, Tim. They have been happily married for forty-two years. She is a mother of four grown children and has six grandchildren. She is involved in inner-healing prayer ministry at her church. She and her husband enjoy camping along the California coast and spending time with their grandchildren.

ANGEL GLIMPSES

When we compare the stories of angel encounters found in the Old Testament with those in the New Testament, we find striking and compelling similarities. In both Testaments:

- Angels guide and direct believers.
- Angels are depicted as guardians who protect believers from harm.
- Angels deliver God's messages, provide instruction, and predict the future.
- Angels are sent by God to humans to prepare hearts, to commission them for special ministries, and to encourage them.

Angels were active in the lives of believers in both the Old Testament and the New Testament. There is no reason to conclude angels are less active in the lives of believers today. Throughout sacred history, angels have been God's ministers, sent to serve those who are heirs of salvation, and the same is true today. Angels are all around us. We can rely on the God of angels each and every day.[27]

CHAPTER NINETEEN

SAFE INSIDE

AMBER HORSMAN

The day was a typical Saturday in South Chicago, Illinois, featuring gangs, gunshots, and a lone seminary student making his rounds to the families who attended church with him. Bro. McSpadden walked without fear through the streets, knocking on doors and praying with folks.

He rounded the last corner to visit the last home. As he walked up the stairs to the second-story apartment, a worried woman came rushing out to meet him.

"Oh, Brother Mac! Brother Mac! I'm so glad you've come! I think something is terribly wrong with my son." She pulled Bro. McSpadden up the last few steps and into the small and humble apartment. Two sets of expectant eyes glanced up as their momma came flying through the door with the seminary student.

As he caught his breath, Bro. McSpadden asked, "Mona, whatever is the problem?"

"It's Louie," she said, almost in a whisper. "I think he's seeing things."

Bro. McSpadden looked over at the youngest boy sitting on the floor.

"Two nights ago," Mona said, "we were at home and could hear a fight starting out in the street. I brought the boys into the house and locked the door. Oh! It was terrible, Brother Mac! There were gunshots and shouting. We could hear all of it! Then, suddenly, we heard someone coming up the stairs and banging on the doors."

Mona's eyes went wide as she continued. "Then came a terrible pounding on *our* door! The whole room shook, and the door handle rattled. I grabbed Stevie and called for Louie, but Louie would not come! He sat right in the middle of the floor, playing. I was screaming for him to come hide in the bedroom with us, but he just wouldn't. He looked at me and said, 'Momma, it's okay. This man is gonna protect us.' But Brother McSpadden, there was no one else here! Not a soul."

Mona sank into an old, worn-out chair. "I don't think Louie would lie to me, but what if he's going crazy?" She dropped her head into her hands and sighed.

Bro. McSpadden walked over to Louie, crossed his legs, and sat beside the boy. "Louie, who was in the room with you when your momma was hiding in the bedroom?"

Louie looked up. "I don't know his name. But he was a really big man—the biggest I've ever seen—and all dressed in white. He said he would protect us and I didn't need to be scared."

"Is he still here?" asked Bro. McSpadden.

"No. He was just here while the fight was happ'in."

Bro. McSpadden smiled and stood. "Mona, you've got nothing to worry about. Louie saw an angel. God sent an angel to protect you."

Mona shook her head. "Then why couldn't I see him?"

"Mona, what would you have done if you'd seen a big man in the apartment during all that? You probably would have freaked out even more. You would not have thought he was here to protect you."

Mona looked relieved. "You mean we had an angel here the whole time?"

Bro. McSpadden nodded. "It would make sense. The Bible does talk about the faith of a child. Louie has the faith to believe, and he witnessed the guardian angel God sent."

Mona smiled and thanked Bro. McSpadden profusely. He prayed with the family and invited them to church in the morning.

As Bro. McSpadden walked away, he smiled to himself. *Oh, to have the faith of a child.*

Amber Horsman reports that this is a true story from her father's life. The names of the family members have been changed, but Bro. McSpadden still serves as a pastor in Rochester, Indiana. Amber Horsman is his oldest daughter and is married to a pastor herself. She has one young son and enjoys writing and serving in her local church.

To find out more about these and other miraculous stories please visit http://www.WhenGodHappens.com for:

Exclusive video interviews with the storytellers
Premium content and free stories
Ongoing God Stories blog
To share **your** miracle story

ENDNOTES

1. Tan, Paul Lee. *Encyclopedia of 7700 Illustrations: Signs of the Times.* (Garland, TX: Bible Communications, Inc., 1996).
2. Charles R. Swindoll and Roy B. Zuck. *Understanding Christian Theology* (Nashville, TN: Thomas Nelson Publishers, 2003).
3. Arnold G. Fruchtenbaum. *The Messianic Bible Study Collection.* Vol. 73 (Tustin, CA: Ariel Ministries, 1983).
4. A. Colin Day. *Collins Thesaurus of the Bible* (Bellingham, WA: Logos Bible Software, 2009).
5. Wayne A. Grudem. *Systematic Theology: An Introduction to Biblical Doctrine* (Leicester, England: Inter-Varsity Press, 2004).
6. Elizabeth Elliot. *A Slow and Certain Light* (Waco, TX: Word Books, 1973).
7. Tyndale House Publishers. *Holy Bible: New Living Translation* (Carol Stream, IL: Tyndale House Publishers, 2013).
8. Charles R. Swindoll and Roy B. Zuck. *Understanding Christian Theology* (Nashville, TN: Thomas Nelson Publishers, 2003).
9. Paul Lee Tan. *Encyclopedia of 7700 Illustrations: Signs of the Times* (Garland, TX: Bible Communications, Inc., 1996).
10. Robert J. Morgan. *Nelson's Complete Book of Stories, Illustrations, and Quotes.* electronic ed (Nashville, TN: Thomas Nelson Publishers, 2000).

11. Billy Graham. *Angels: God's Secret Agents* (Waco, TX: Word Books, 1986), 3.

12. C. S. Lewis. *Screwtape Letters* (New York: The Macmillan Company, 1961).

13. Robert J. Morgan. *Nelson's Complete Book of Stories, Illustrations, and Quotes.* electronic ed (Nashville, TN: Thomas Nelson Publishers, 2000).

14. Darlene Deibler Rose. *Evidence Not Seen: A Woman's Miraculous Faith in the Jungles of World War II* (Carlisle, United Kingdom: OM Publishing, 1988), 46.

15. This story previously appeared in *The One Year Experiencing God's Love Devotional*, published by Tyndale House, 2017.

16. Pieced together from several books and internet articles about the *Titanic*. His story also appeared in the *Congressional Record* of the investigation of the sinking of the *Titanic*.

17. Robert J. Morgan. *Nelson's Complete Book of Stories, Illustrations, and Quotes.* electronic ed (Nashville: Thomas Nelson Publishers, 2000).

18. Larry D. Wright, "To Illustrate," *Leadership Journal*, Spring Quarter, 1988. Attributed to a newsletter, *Our America*.

19. A. T. Pierson. *The Gospel: Its Heart, Heights, and Hopes.* Vol. 1 (Grand Rapids, MI: Baker Book House, 1978), 9.

20. Kenneth Boa and William Proctor. *The Return of the Star of Bethlehem* (Garden City, NY: Doubleday, 1980), 123. See also Zuck, *Precious in His Sight*, 185–87.

21. James Arthur Woychuck, "The Biblical Relationship Between Stars and Angels" (Th.M. thesis, Dallas Theological Seminary, 1996).

22. Charles R. Swindoll and Roy B. Zuck. *Understanding Christian Theology* (Nashville, TN: Thomas Nelson Publishers, 2003).

23. Larry Richards. *Every Angel in the Bible* Everything in the Bible Series. (Nashville, TN: T. Nelson, 1997).

24. Charles Haddon Spurgeon. *Spurgeon's Sermons.* Vol. 2 (Grand Rapids, MI: Baker Book House, 1983), 191.

25. Lewis Sperry Chafer, "Angelology." *Bibliotheca Sacra* 98 (Dallas, TX: Dallas Theological Seminary, 1941): 415.

26. Martin Luther. *The Table Talk of Martin Luther,* ed. Thomas S. Kepler (Grand Rapids, MI: Baker, 1952), 279–280.

27. Larry Richards. *Every Angel in the Bible.* Everything in the Bible Series (Nashville, TN: T. Nelson, 1997).